Cultural Appropriation

M. M. Eboch, Book Editor

GREENHAVEN
PUBLISHING

Published in 2020 by Greenhaven Publishing, LLC
353 3rd Avenue, Suite 255, New York, NY 10010

Copyright © 2020 by Greenhaven Publishing, LLC

First Edition

Articles in Greenhaven Publishing anthologies are often edited for length to meet page requirements. In addition, original titles of these works are changed to clearly present the main thesis and to explicitly indicate the author's opinion. Every effort is made to ensure that Greenhaven Publishing accurately reflects the original intent of the authors. Every effort has been made to trace the owners of the copyrighted material.

Library of Congress Cataloging-in-Publication Data

Names: Eboch, M. M., editor.
Title: Cultural appropriation / M. M. Eboch, book editor.
Description: New York : Greenhaven Publishing, [2020] | Series: Introducing issues with opposing viewpoints | Audience: Grade level 7-12. | Includes bibliographical references and index.
Identifiers: LCCN 2018053309| ISBN 9781534505667 (library bound) | ISBN 9781534505674 (pbk.)
Subjects: LCSH: Acculturation. | Cultural appropriation. | Postcolonialism—Social aspects.
Classification: LCC HM841 .C76 2019 | DDC 303.48/2—dc23
LC record available at https://lccn.loc.gov/2018053309

Manufactured in the United States of America

Website: http://greenhavenpublishing.com

FEBRUARY 2021

Contents

Chapter 3: Who Is Harmed by Cultural Appropriation and How?

Foreword

Indulging in a wide spectrum of ideas, beliefs, and perspectives is a critical cornerstone of democracy. After all, it is often debates over differences of opinion, such as whether to legalize abortion, how to treat prisoners, or when to enact the death penalty, that shape our society and drive it forward. Such diversity of thought is frequently regarded as the hallmark of a healthy and civilized culture. As the Reverend Clifford Schutjer of the First Congregational Church in Mansfield, Ohio, declared in a 2001 sermon, "Surrounding oneself with only like-minded people, restricting what we listen to or read only to what we find agreeable is irresponsible. Refusing to entertain doubts once we make up our minds is a subtle but deadly form of arrogance." With this advice in mind, Introducing Issues with Opposing Viewpoints books aim to open readers' minds to the critically divergent views that comprise our world's most important debates.

Introducing Issues with Opposing Viewpoints simplifies for students the enormous and often overwhelming mass of material now available via print and electronic media. Collected in every volume is an array of opinions that captures the essence of a particular controversy or topic. Introducing Issues with Opposing Viewpoints books embody the spirit of nineteenth-century journalist Charles A. Dana's axiom: "Fight for your opinions, but do not believe that they contain the whole truth, or the only truth." Absorbing such contrasting opinions teaches students to analyze the strength of an argument and compare it to its opposition. From this process readers can inform and strengthen their own opinions, or be exposed to new information that will change their minds. Introducing Issues with Opposing Viewpoints is a mosaic of different voices. The authors are statesmen, pundits, academics, journalists, corporations, and ordinary people who have felt compelled to share their experiences and ideas in a public forum. Their words have been collected from newspapers, journals, books, speeches, interviews, and the Internet, the fastest growing body of opinionated material in the world.

Introducing Issues with Opposing Viewpoints shares many of the well-known features of its critically acclaimed parent series, Opposing

Viewpoints. The articles allow readers to absorb and compare divergent perspectives. Active reading questions preface each viewpoint, requiring the student to approach the material thoughtfully and carefully. Photographs, charts, and graphs supplement each article. A thorough introduction provides readers with crucial background on an issue. An annotated bibliography points the reader toward articles, books, and websites that contain additional information on the topic. An appendix of organizations to contact contains a wide variety of charities, nonprofit organizations, political groups, and private enterprises that each hold a position on the issue at hand. Finally, a comprehensive index allows readers to locate content quickly and efficiently.

Introducing Issues with Opposing Viewpoints is also significantly different from Opposing Viewpoints. As the series title implies, its presentation will help introduce students to the concept of opposing viewpoints and teach them to use this material to aid in critical writing and debate. The series' four-color, accessible format makes the books attractive and inviting to readers of all levels. In addition, each viewpoint has been carefully edited to maximize a reader's understanding of the content. Short but thorough viewpoints capture the essence of an argument. A substantial, thought-provoking essay question placed at the end of each viewpoint asks the student to further investigate the issues raised in the viewpoint, compare and contrast two authors' arguments, or consider how one might go about forming an opinion on the topic at hand. Each viewpoint contains sidebars that include at-a-glance information and handy statistics. A Facts About section located in the back of the book further supplies students with relevant facts and figures.

Following in the tradition of the Opposing Viewpoints series, Greenhaven Publishing continues to provide readers with invaluable exposure to the controversial issues that shape our world. As John Stuart Mill once wrote: "The only way in which a human being can make some approach to knowing the whole of a subject is by hearing what can be said about it by persons of every variety of opinion and studying all modes in which it can be looked at by every character of mind. No wise man ever acquired his wisdom in any mode but this." It is to this principle that Introducing Issues with Opposing Viewpoints books are dedicated.

Introduction

"Are we, Westerners, liberal Westerners, too over-sensitive of the feelings of others brought on by white guilt? Or are we right to call out what we think is wrong when we see it? Should we wait before speaking, to see what the actual people affected think? Or is it our duty to step in first?"
—David Barnett, The Independent

What is your culture? Where does it come from?

Five hundred years ago, separating and classifying cultures was easier. Most countries had a clearly identifiable culture: food, music, dances, art forms, clothing, and hairstyles. Within a country, you might find variations based on region, ethnic group, religion, and maybe even class. But most people had a culture that they had inherited from their parents, grandparents, and more distant ancestors. That culture helped people know who they were and how they fit into the world. Any change happened very slowly.

Our world is more complex today. Worldwide, over 250 million people live in a country other than the one where they were born. More than 40 million people living in the United States were born in another country. Immigrants and the children of immigrants together make up about 27 percent of the US population. Nearly everyone living in America has immigrant ancestors within a dozen generations. The census identifies only about one percent of the population as indigenous Native American. Everyone else had their culture handed down from somewhere else.

So what is American culture? Who gets to define it? Is it fast-food hamburgers, suburbs, and long commutes? Yoga pants and lattes? Soul food and hip-hop? Bodegas and taco trucks? A choice between sushi, Chinese takeout, Thai food, and Indian buffet, depending on your mood? All of the above and much more?

Many people have brought their native cultures to America, but over time aspects of culture shift, blend, and adapt. For example, African American music draws on the roots of people who were transported from various African countries and enslaved in the

United States. Their early folk music and spirituals developed into blues, jazz, gospel, soul, rock, and later hip-hop and rap. "Soul food" originated in the limited rations enslaved people got in the Deep South. Today some soul food restaurants have gone upscale, others have gone vegan, and variations can be found in cities from New York to Los Angeles. Health-conscious cooks might trade frying for baking and pork products for smoked turkey. Culture changes over time, even when people stay in the same place.

Meanwhile, the world's culture is available in seconds over the internet. If you want to listen to Korean pop music or find a recipe for Peruvian seafood soup, you can. It's also much easier to visit other countries for vacations, schooling, or temporary work stays.

Many benefits come from this cultural exchange. When groups share their cultures, people understand each other better. Friendships can arise. New art forms can develop. People get to enjoy a broader world, full of cultural delights.

So if sharing culture is good, why are people throwing around accusations of cultural appropriation, as if that's a bad thing?

White celebrities have been criticized for wearing their hair in cornrows, a traditionally black hairstyle with roots in Africa. Fashion designers have been condemned for putting white models in Native American headdresses or Sikh turbans. Protesters have demanded that sports teams such as the Cleveland Indians baseball team and the Washington Redskins football team change their names. A United Nations meeting even started discussing whether cultural appropriation should be illegal worldwide.

Accusations of cultural appropriation have hit ordinary individuals as well. Halloween costumes are a particular sore point. On college campuses, students are sometimes warned not to wear costumes based on stereotypes of a different cultural group. Some critics feel that white people should never wear items from other cultures. They say it's stealing from that culture, and whites have already stolen enough and destroyed enough.

And then there are those who think the whole debate has gone too far. Doesn't freedom of speech mean we can wear whatever we want? Anyway, life would be boring if we only stuck to our own culture. One of the wonders of our modern age is that we can try different ethnic foods, listen to a wide variety of world music, and even read books and watch movies from other countries. Now we're supposed to stay in our own little boxes? No fair!

Those who have explored the issue fully often say the matter comes down to cultural exchange versus cultural appropriation. Cultural exchange is positive, with two cultures equally sharing and celebrating each other. The negative connotation of cultural appropriation comes from a power imbalance. The person doing the appropriating comes from a dominant group. In America, that typically means white people. White people have a long history of taking from less powerful groups. They benefit, while the weaker group suffers.

This happened when early European immigrants took land from the people who already lived on the continent. It happened when white rockers grew rich and famous for making popular the music developed by black musicians. It still goes on today. It happens in fashion, when white models show off designs by white designers who draw on different cultural groups without asking permission, giving credit, or sharing the profits. It happens when a white celebrity is praised for being trendy and fashionable for wearing a bindi, while a Hindu woman wearing the traditional mark is told to "act American" or get out. This double standard or power imbalance lies at the heart of cultural appropriation. It's taking without asking, and without giving anything in return. Cultural exchange is a fair trade, while cultural appropriation is theft.

It may seem like the only safe answer is to avoid ever venturing outside one's own culture. But most people who have examined the issue say there's another answer. The key is intent. It's perfectly acceptable for people to explore other cultures respectfully. They should try to understand the history and meaning behind clothing or accessories with religious or spiritual significance. They should only buy Native American jewelry from Native Americans, to make sure the money goes back to the people who created the art form. They should recognize the contradiction when black culture is celebrated in music and fashion, but black people are subjected to racism. They should ask questions, ask permission, and give credit where it's due. They should recognize privilege when they have it, and work to make everyone equal.

That sounds complicated, especially when all you want to do is enjoy a burrito on Cinco de Mayo. Culture isn't simple anymore. But maybe the trade-offs are worth the trouble. The current debates are explored in *Introducing Issues with Opposing Viewpoints: Cultural Appropriation*, shedding light on this ongoing contemporary issue.

Chapter 1

Cultural Exchange, Cultural Appropriation, and Privilege

Singer Katy Perry was criticized for cultural appropriation when she performed dressed as a geisha.

What Is Cultural Appropriation?

Neil Van Leeuwen

"There is no way to understand the concept of cultural appropriation without understanding the historical background of colonialism."

In the following viewpoint, Neil Van Leeuwen explores the meaning of cultural appropriation. He notes that using something from another culture is not always a problem. However, it can be. Sometimes people in a dominant culture use something from another culture without asking. People in the marginalized culture may feel hurt or disrespected. The imbalance of power between the groups causes the problem. Van Leeuwen is associate professor of philosophy at Georgia State University.

AS YOU READ, CONSIDER THE FOLLOWING QUESTIONS:
1. What holiday does the author use as a starting point in exploring cultural appropriation?
2. Why is colonialism essential to understanding cultural appropriation according to the viewpoint?
3. What is the moral vice in cultural appropriation according to the author?

"What is Cultural Appropriation?" by Neil Van Leeuwen, Philosophy Talk, October 27, 2015. Reprinted by permission.

This Halloween we'll see kids, college students, and other revelers dressed in costumes ranging from scary to hilarious: Chewbaccas, spandex police officers, Harry Potters, Frodos ... even Elvis. But at any party, we have a good chance of seeing cultural appropriation. We might see white people glibly dressed in mock Native American headdresses, frat brothers dressing "ghetto," people who have no real connection to India wearing red dots on their foreheads, would-be Zulus, Geishas (from Texas), and of course a gringo in a sombrero.

Such mimicry has come under increasing condemnation recently, and probably for good reasons. But, we might wonder, what exactly is wrong with it? And how precisely should we define "cultural appropriation" anyway?

On the basis of the examples above, we might say cultural appropriation is use or mimicry of artifacts or manners from another culture without permission from any members of that culture.

But it's not hard to see that this definition won't do.

It implies, wrongly, that every time someone from one culture uses an idea from another culture, without explicitly asking, that "cultural appropriation" has occurred. But I don't think, for example, someone who goes to France and then comes home and makes crepes should be called a "cultural appropriator." (In some weak sense, sure, but that's not the sense we're after.) Nor should someone who visits China and learns how to use chopsticks or how to sing a song they heard on the radio.

Much if not most culture (good and bad) results from different cultures bumping into each other and borrowing or just absorbing ideas. So if we're to talk about "cultural appropriation"—as opposed to just "culture"—we have to mean something more.

So the definition above is an instructive failure. I think many people would be tempted to define "cultural appropriation" in this fashion. But we've seen that it wrongly includes mere cultural influences and instances of learning that are in no way problematic. What next?

It seems to me that there is no way to understand the concept of cultural appropriation properly without understanding the historical background of colonialism. Colonialism was and is the systematic subjugation of one group of people by another, where that subjugation is motivated and rationalized by racist ideology. Examples of this have occurred throughout Asia, Africa, and the Americas, usually with Europeans as the aggressors, though Chinese, Japanese, and Ottoman empires have historically established colonies as well.

In my view, it's the latter component of colonialism, the racist ideology, that is crucial for understanding what cultural appropriation really is. I think anything worth applying the term "cultural appropriation" to will be something that expresses at least a psychological vestige of a racist ideology that figured in one of the large-scale colonialist projects.

Racist ideologies characteristically portray an entire group of people, a race or ethnicity, as simplistic, naïve, lazy, untrustworthy, or violent. And such portrayal, embedded in the mind in the form of stereotypes, is used in colonialist contexts to rationalize more brutal forms of mistreatment and ultimately appropriation of much more than just culture.

So this is what differentiates merely using chopsticks to eat (which is not cultural appropriation in any interesting sense) from dressing up for Halloween like a "Chinese" guy from a bad Kung Fu movie (definitely cultural appropriation). In the latter case, the non-Chinese person wearing the outfit expresses—typically unwittingly—a psychological tendency, a tendency to think of another person as a simpler kind of creature than oneself. Furthermore, it is a tendency to think of a whole class of other people in simplifying terms. This psychological tendency is the vestige, or one manifestation of it, that I referred to above.

So a more accurate definition of "cultural appropriation" goes like this: cultural appropriation is where people from a group that oppressed or oppresses another group mimics or represents cultural artifacts or manners of the oppressed group in a way that expresses or reinforces psychological elements of the racist ideology inherent in

Is it morally wrong for a white woman to wear her hair in dreadlocks?

the colonialist project responsible for the oppression. Such appropriating mimicry can take many forms, but what unifies them will be an implicit or explicit view of other people that makes them out to be less than what they are.

Is cultural appropriation inherently morally wrong? Or is it merely stupid and abrasive? The progenitor of cultural appropriation, colonialism, was and is certainly morally wrong, without question. But does the same go for the mere putting on of a silly Halloween costume?

The details of any given case will matter. Furthermore, I think this is an area where it's better to think in continuous terms of morally better and worse, rather than wrong or not wrong simpliciter. A European's going to a Halloween party in a traditional Congolese suit they somehow acquired may not be a gross moral transgression, though it might make us morally uneasy. But whatever its moral status, going in blackface is clearly much, much worse.

The moral vice, when there is vice, consists in perpetuating components of a racist ideology that, in more pronounced forms, motivates and rationalizes much more significant harms. We may grant that one outfit on one occasion might not do much more harm than leaving a few people seriously annoyed. But it signals to members of one's group—the currently or historically oppressing group—that certain patterns of thought about another group are okay, even something to be enjoyed. Against the background of such signaling, more coordinated aggression can emerge.

These thoughts may all seem too weighty to be about what to wear to your next Halloween party. And perhaps in some way they are. But the psychological fact of implicit racism and other forms of prejudice are by now well known. Given that, the correct thought is that it's better morally safe than morally sorry.

In any case, you can always be Chewbacca, Harry Potter, or a cop in spandex. You'll then be merely silly, but perhaps that's a good thing.

EVALUATING THE AUTHOR'S ARGUMENTS:

Viewpoint author Neil Van Leeuwen presents several arguments about cultural appropriation. How will you think about Halloween costumes in the future, based on the context he uses to frame his argument?

We All Should Be Aware of the Ways in Which We Are Privileged

Ruth De Souza

"If you see yourself as a 'good' person then it is painful to be 'called out,' and see yourself as a bad person."

In the following excerpted viewpoint, Ruth De Souza argues that when people are unaware of their privilege, they often unintentionally support a racist society. On the other hand, people who are aware of their privilege can use their power to help others. People can be privileged in some areas and not in others. This means almost everyone has some form of privilege. De Souza is a research fellow and former leader of research, policy, and evaluation at the Centre for Culture, Ethnicity and Health in Australia.

AS YOU READ, CONSIDER THE FOLLOWING QUESTIONS:
1. What aspects of identity can be considered in terms of privilege?
2. How can someone be contributing to racism even if they are not themselves actively racist?
3. What is intersectionality?

"What is privilege and cultural appropriation? and why is it so difficult to talk about?" by Ruth De Souza, Centre of Culture, Ethnicty & Health, February 17, 2016. Reprinted by permission.

The concept of privilege originally developed in relation to analyses of race and gender but has expanded to include social class, ability level, sexuality and other aspects of identity.

Many people have really strong reactions to these concepts—why is that?

Robin DiAngelo, professor of multicultural education and author of *What Does it Mean to Be White? Developing White Racial Literacy*, developed the term "white fragility" to identify:

> *a state in which even a minimum amount of racial stress becomes intolerable, triggering a range of defensive moves. These moves include outward display of emotions such as anger, fear and guilt, and behaviors such as argumentation, silence and leaving the stress-inducing situation*

DiAngelo suggests that for white people, racism or oppression are viewed as something that bad or immoral people do. The racist is the person who is verbally abusive toward people of color on public transport, or a former racist state like apartheid South Africa. If you see yourself as a "good" person then it is painful to be "called out," and see yourself as a bad person. Iris Marion Young's work is useful. She conceptualises oppression in the Foucauldian sense as:

> *the disadvantage and injustice some people suffer not because of a tyrannical power coerces them but because of the everyday practices of a well-intentioned liberal society…*

Young points out the actions of many people going about their daily lives contribute to the maintenance and reproduction of oppression, even as few would view themselves as agents of oppression. We cannot avoid oppression, as it is structural and woven throughout the system, rather than reflecting a few people's choices or policies. Its causes are embedded in the unquestioned norms, habits, symbols and assumptions underlying institutional rules and the collective consequences of following those rules (Young, 1990). Seeing oppression as the practices of a well intentioned liberal society removes the focus from individual acts that might repress the actions of others to

Because of their inherent privilege, white people might not understand how dressing up in another person's cultural costume can be tone deaf.

acknowledging that "powerful norms and hierarchies of both privilege and injustice are built into our everyday practices" (Henderson & Waterstone, 2008, p.52). These hierarchies call for structural rather than individual remedies.

We probably need to start with privilege— what does that term mean?

McIntosh identified how she had obtained unearned privileges in society just by being White and defined white privilege as:

> *an invisible package of unearned assets which I can count on cashing in each day, but about which I am meant to remain oblivious (p. 1).*

Her essay prompted understanding of how one's success is largely attributable to one's arbitrarily assigned social location in society, rather than the outcome of individual effort. She suggested that white people benefit from historical and contemporary forms of racism (the inequitable distribution and exercise of power among ethnic groups) and that these discriminate or disadvantage people of color.

How does privilege relate to racism, sexism? Are they the same thing?

It's useful to view the "isms" in the context of institutional power, a point illustrated by Sian Ferguson:

> In a patriarchal society, women do not have institutional power (at least, not based on their gender). In a white supremacist society, people of color don't have race-based institutional power.

[...]

Without context white people are socialized to remain oblivious to their unearned advantages and view them as earned through merit. Increasingly the term privilege is being used outside of social justice settings to the arts. In a critique of the Hottest 100 list in Australia Erin Riley points out that the dominance of straight, white male voices which crowds out women, Indigenous Australians, immigrants and people of diverse sexual and gender identities. These groups are marginalised and the centrality of white men maintained, reducing the opportunity for empathy towards people with other experiences.

Do we all have some sort of privilege?

Yes, depending on the context. The concept of intersectionality by Kimberlé Crenshaw is useful, it suggests that people can be privileged in some ways and not others. For example as a migrant and a woman of color I experience certain disadvantages but as a middle class cis-gendered, able-bodied woman with a PhD and without an accent (only a Kiwi one which is indulged) I experience other advantages that ease my passage through the world.

How does an awareness of privilege change the way a society works?

You might have also seen or heard the phrase "check your privilege" which is a way of asking someone to think about their own privilege and how they might monitor it in a social setting. Exposing color blindness and challenging the assumption of race-neutrality is one mechanism for addressing the issue of privilege and its obverse oppression. Increasingly in health and social care, emphasis is being placed on critiquing how our own positions contribute to inequality (see my chapter on cultural safety), and developing ethical and moral commitments to addressing racism so that equality and justice can be made possible. As Christine Emba notes "There's no way to level the playing field unless we first can all see how uneven it is." One of the ways this can be done is through experiencing exercises like the Privilege Walk which you can watch on video. Jenn Sutherland-Miller in Medium reflects on her experience of it and proposes that:

> Instead of privilege being the thing that gives me a leg up, it becomes the thing I use to give others a leg up. Privilege becomes a way to create equality and inclusion, to right old wrongs, to demand justice on a daily basis and to create the dialogue that will grow our society forward.

Is privilege something we can change?

If we move beyond guilt and paralysis we can use our privilege to build solidarity and challenge oppression. Audra Williams points out that a genuine display of solidarity can require making a personal sacrifice. Citing the example of Aziz Ansari's Master of None, where in challenging the director of a commercial about the lack of women with speaking roles, he ends up not being in the commercial at all when it is re-written with speaking roles for women. Ultimately privilege does not get undone through "confession" but through collective work to dismantle oppressive systems as Andrea Smith writes.

Cultural appropriation is a different concept, but an understanding of privilege is important, what is cultural appropriation?

Cultural appropriation is when somebody adopts aspects of a culture that is not their own (Nadra Kareem Little). Usually it is a charge levelled at people from the dominant culture to signal power dynamic, where elements have been taken from a culture of people who have been systematically oppressed by the dominant group. Most critics of the concept are white (see white fragility). Kimberly Chabot Davis proposes that white co-optation or cultural consumption and commodification, can be cross-cultural encounters that can foster empathy and lead to working against privilege among white people. I think that it is always important to ask permission and talk to people from that culture first rather than assuming it is okay to use.

[...]

Can someone from a less privileged culture appropriate from the more privileged culture?

No, marginalized people often have to adopt elements of the dominant culture in order to survive conditions that make life more of a struggle if they don't.

Does an object or symbol have to have some religious or special cultural significance to be appropriated?

Appropriation is harmful for a number of reasons including making things "cool" for White people that would be denigrated in People of Color. For example Fatima Farha observes that when Hindu women in the United States wear the bindi, they are often made fun of, or seen as traditional or backward but when someone from the dominant culture wears such items they are called exotic and beautiful.

[...]

In essence as Ijeoma Oluo points out cultural appropriation is a symptom, not the cause, of an oppressive and exploitative world order which involves stealing the work of those less privileged. Really valuing people involves valuing their culture and taking the time to acknowledge its historical and social context. Valuing isn't just appreciation but also considering whether the appropriation of intellectual property results in economic benefits for the people who created it. Kareem Abdul-Jabbar suggests that it is often one way:

One very legitimate point is economic. In general, when blacks create something that is later adopted by white culture, white people tend to make a lot more money from it… It feels an awful lot like slavery to have others profit from your efforts.

Loving burritos doesn't make someone less racist against Latinos. Lusting after Bo Derek in 10 doesn't make anyone appreciate black culture more… Appreciating an individual item from a culture doesn't translate into accepting the whole people. While high-priced cornrows on a white celebrity on the red carper at the Oscars is chic, those same cornrows on the little black girl in Watts, Los Angeles, are a symbol of her ghetto lifestyle. A white person looking black gets a fashion spread in a glossy magazine; a black person wearing the same thing gets pulled over by the police. One can understand the frustration.

The appropriative process is also selective, as Greg Tate observes in *Everything but the burden*, where African American cultural properties including music, food, fashion, hairstyles, dances are sold as American to the rest of the world but with the black presence erased from it. The only thing not stolen is the burden of the denial of human rights and economic opportunity. Appropriation can be ambivalent, as seen in the desire to simultaneously possess and erase black culture.

[…]

EVALUATING THE AUTHOR'S ARGUMENTS:

In this viewpoint, Ruth De Souza suggests that someone with privilege can use the power for good. Did the author make you want to examine your privilege and use it for good? Why or why not?

People of Color Can Culturally Appropriate Too

"*The key here was that we were active participants in celebrating each other, not erasing each other.*"

Fatimah Asghar

In the following viewpoint Fatimah Asghar claims that people of color can appropriate from each other. She notes that sometimes sharing culture is a way of building bonds or joining a community. In addition, different cultures may share the same practices. Yet sometimes cultural appropriation is problematic between people of color. When something is done to look pretty or be cool, it's problematic, she says. Fatimah Asghar is a poet, screenwriter, educator and performer.

AS YOU READ, CONSIDER THE FOLLOWING QUESTIONS:
1. Is it different when people of color appropriate from each other's cultures, as opposed to when white people appropriate from another culture?
2. Why is it important to understand the history of a symbol before wearing it, according to this author?
3. Is it all right to participate in another culture's traditions when you are invited to do so, according to the author?

"Can People of Color Culturally Appropriate? Yes. BUT… ," by Fatimah Asghar, Originally Published in Black Girl Dangerous, BGD Press, Inc,, September 8, 2015. Reprinted by permission.

Lets face it, cultural appropriation sucks. We've all seen white people with dreads stomping around like they own the place, or drunk hipsters at music festivals with headdresses and bindis. As people of color it can be incredibly frustrating to see things like this. It reminds us that we live in a world in which whiteness continues to steal cultures without regard to the actual people who've invented or maintained those cultures.

Cultural appropriation occurs when members of a dominant group take elements and symbols of another culture for their own economic or social gain while simultaneously devaluing and silencing the bodies, opinions and voices of the oppressed culture.

This is problematic for a lot of reasons, and triggering for people of color because it reinforces the way imperialism and racism have allowed the white Western world to steal and exploit people of color while simultaneously denying us representation and rights.

Since most things regarding race in the US are thought of in terms of their relationship to whiteness, it's easy for people of color to spot when white people are appropriating our cultures. It's harder to examine the ways that we borrow from, steal from, and erase each other.

So, can people of color appropriate from each other?

1. Yes, we can. But:
2. Sometimes people call things appropriation without understanding that multiple cultures engage in the same practices and have shared practices for centuries.

While all groups of color face our own unique problems that grow with intersecting identities (gender, sexuality, class, etc) we all face a lack of representation and the repercussions of negative stereotypes in America. This is reinforced and evidenced in many ways, such as the creation of the model-minority myth of Asians in America, colorism (discrimination based on the pigmentation of your skin and the belief that lighter skin is better), or hierarchy among immigrant generations and who is considered "more American."

When we take from each other, we might be assimilating into our neighborhoods or schools or community in order to be accepted by them.

It is a mistake to think that people of color are immune to appropriating culture themselves. But the issue is complicated.

Because many communities of color are set next to each other in the US, we often end up in a series of cultural exchanges that can be mutually respectful and important to our survival or negotiating of America. My friends of color would often hang out with me for Eid and dress up in our traditional clothes. We constantly exchanged food and recipes. I would go to their houses for Easter, Christmas, and Kwanza and participate in all of the rituals that came along with those holidays. The key here was that we were active participants in celebrating each other, not erasing each other. We were invited by each other to participate in customs, not just donning them because we thought they looked or sounded cool. We also weren't gaining social or economic capital from partaking in each other's cultures.

As people of color, many of us come from painful legacies of immigration, slavery, and exploitation. There is a violent erasure and orphaning that we have to deal with as we negotiate America. My experience has taught me that I am not considered American even though I was born here. I don't speak Urdu fluently, am not well versed on the current politics of Pakistan, but cling to elements of my Pakistani and Kashmiri culture and sometimes romanticize them. I rock saris anytime I can and wear kameezes as dresses. I do my research before I wear something, but a lot of time that comes from

the Internet and not from some deep cultural exchange in my family. That might be considered by some to be appropriative, but for me and other individuals of diasporic identity, it is a necessary part of survival and sanity in America.

My South Asian friends have complained about seeing other people of color rocking bindis or shalwaar kameez and called them appropriative. Yes, it hurts us to see our culture trivialized or worn as an easily dispensable fashion accessory, especially when it wasn't seen as cool to wear those things growing up. However, it ignores the incredibly complex and rich history of exchange between East and North Africa and South Asia. Though bindis have an important place in Hinduism, they are not only a symbol of Hindu spirituality, but also have important symbolic value and origin in Africa. Therefore, people of the African diaspora have the cultural right to wear bindis in the same way people of the South Asian diaspora have that right.

So next time you are quick to call out someone for culturally appropriating, ask yourself:

- Do I know the full history of this symbol? Is it used in other cultures as well?
- Do I know the identity of the person who I am accusing of being problematic, or am I assuming their identity?
- By using or doing this symbol, is this person benefiting from it socially or economically while erasing the people who made it?

This isn't to say that people of color can't be problematic or appropriative. Cultural exchange is important to know, but sometimes people can just f*** up and are appropriative.

We can do this by exoticizing other cultures, and like whiteness, taking while erasing the bodies of others. For example, wearing Indigenous American headdresses because its "cool" or "pretty" when we are not Indigenous American (such as Pharrell Williams wearing a headdress). The erasure of Indigenous American bodies and culture is not figurative, but very literally enacted by the systematic genocide of indigenous people. Even if we (or our people) were not the ones to have orchestrated this systematic genocide, we live on stolen land and might be complicit in their erasure.

This is also true for the pervasive anti-blackness in Asian, Latino, and Indigenous cultures—the way that we can appropriate slang, dress, and black cultures while simultaneously erasing black people. Or the ways that we can benefit off of black civil rights struggle without contributing to it or fighting against anti-blackness.

Here are some guiding questions to ask yourself when you wonder if you are appropriating:

- Why do I want to do this? Is it to be cool? Because it looks pretty? (Heads up: if it's just to be cool or look pretty, it's probably problematic)
- Is this a symbol of a political statement? If so, do I align with the politics not in just dress and appearance, but in actual struggle and resistance?
- Do I know the history of this symbol or where it comes from?
- Have I been invited by a member of this community to participate in this culture, word, or symbol?
- What role has this symbol played in my own life?
- Why do I feel entitled to this symbol?

When we approach each other with respect for cultures and struggles as well as the awareness that communities of color have historically been reliant on each other for survival in America, we are much more likely to be able to define the line of respect and appropriation. We can question and examine our own choices rather than assuming that we should have access to everything.

EVALUATING THE AUTHOR'S ARGUMENTS:

Previous viewpoints have suggested that only the dominant culture can appropriate other cultures in a negative way. In the United States, this would mean only white people can appropriate other cultures. Viewpoint author Fatimah Asghar suggests that people of color also can cause harm by appropriating other cultures. Do you agree? How does power come into play when neither culture is the dominant one?

Viewpoint

4

Cultural Exchange Is Fine, but Cultural Appropriation Is Not

"True cultural exchange is not the process of 'Here's my culture, I'll have some of yours' that we sometimes think it is."

Jarune Uwujaren

In the following viewpoint Jarune Uwujaren explores positive cultural exchange versus negative cultural appropriation. She notes that there may not be a clear line between the two. Often it is not simple to answer "Is this thing cultural appropriation?" Education, respect for the culture, and recognizing the imbalance of power are key to finding the answer, she says. Uwujaren is an author at Everyday Feminism, an educational platform that explores issues of gender, sexual orientation, race, class, and other differences.

AS YOU READ, CONSIDER THE FOLLOWING QUESTIONS:

1. Do freedom of speech or personal expression give people the right to wear whatever they want?
2. How is enjoying another culture rather like being a guest in someone's home, according to the author?
3. How is using someone else's cultural symbols for self-expression a form of privilege, according to the author?

"The Difference Between Cultural Exchange and Cultural Appropriation," by Jarune Uwujaren, Everyday Feminism, September 30, 2013. Reprinted by permission.

Cultural appropriation is a term that isn't often heard in daily conversation, which means it's inevitably misunderstood by those who feel attacked by feminists, sociologically-informed bloggers, and others who use the term.

Many a white person sporting dreadlocks or a bindi online has taken cultural appropriation to mean the policing of what white people can or can't wear and enjoy.

Having considered their fashion choices a form of personal expression, some may feel unfairly targeted for simply dressing and acting in a way that feels comfortable for them.

The same can be said for those who find criticisms of the Harlem Shake meme and whatever it is Miley Cyrus did last month to be an obnoxious form of hipsterdom—just because something has origins in black culture, they say, doesn't mean white artists can't emulate and enjoy it.

And then there are people who believe that everything is cultural appropriation—from the passing around of gun powder to the worldwide popularity of tea.

They're tired of certain forms of cultural appropriation—like models in Native American headdresses—being labeled as problematic while many of us are gorging on Chipotle burritos, doing yoga, and popping sushi into our mouths with chopsticks.

They have a point.

Where do we draw the line between "appropriate" forms of cultural exchange and more damaging patterns of cultural appropriation?

To be honest, I don't know that there is a thin, straight line between them.

But even if the line between exchange and appropriation bends, twists, and loop-de-loops in ways it would take decades of academic thought to unpack, it has a definite starting point: Respect.

What Cultural Exchange Is Not

One of the reasons that cultural appropriation is a hard concept to grasp for so many is that Westerners are used to pressing their own culture onto others and taking what they want in return.

Imagine how Native American Indians feel when whites use their heritage as a costume, given their history of subjugation in America.

We tend to think of this as cultural exchange when really, it's no more an exchange than pressuring your neighbors to adopt your ideals while stealing their family heirlooms.

True cultural exchange is not the process of "Here's my culture, I'll have some of yours" that we sometimes think it is. It's something that should be mutual.

Just because Indian Americans wear business suits doesn't mean all Americans own bindis and saris. Just because some black Americans straighten their hair doesn't mean all Americans own dreadlocks.

The fact is, Western culture invites and, at times, demands assimilation. Not every culture has chosen to open itself up to being adopted by outsiders in the same way.

And there's good reason for that.

"Ethnic" clothes and hairstyles are still stigmatized as unprofessional, "cultural" foods are treated as exotic past times, and the vernacular of people of color is ridiculed and demeaned.

So there is an unequal exchange between Western culture—an all-consuming mishmash of over-simplified and sellable foreign influences with a dash each of Coke and Pepsi—and marginalized cultures.

People of all cultures wear business suits and collared shirts to survive. But when one is of the dominant culture, adopting the clothing, food, or slang of other cultures has nothing to do with survival.

So as free as people should be to wear whatever hair and clothing they enjoy, using someone else's cultural symbols to satisfy a personal need for self-expression is an exercise in privilege.

Because for those of us who have felt forced and pressured to change the way we look, behave, and speak just to earn enough respect to stay employed and safe, our modes of self-expression are still limited.

African American Vernacular English (AAVE) is consistently treated as lesser than Standard English, but people whitewash black slang and use expressions they barely understand as punch lines, or to make themselves seem cool.

People shirk "ethnic" clothes in corporate culture, but wear bastardized versions of them on Halloween.

There is no exchange, understanding, or respect in such cases—only taking.

What Cultural Exchange Can Look Like

That doesn't mean that cultural exchange never happens, or that we can never partake in one another's cultures. But there needs to be some element of mutual understanding, equality, and respect for it to be a true exchange.

I remember that at my sister's wedding, the groom—who happened to be white—changed midway through the ceremony along with my sister into modern, but fairly traditional, Nigerian clothes.

Even though some family members found it amusing, there was never any undertone of the clothes being treated as a costume or "experience" for a white person to enjoy for a little bit and discard later. He was invited—both as a new family member and a guest—to engage our culture in this way.

If he had been obnoxious about it—treated it as exotic or weird or pretended he now understood what it means to be Nigerian and refused to wear Western clothes ever again—the experience would have been more appropriative.

But instead, he wore them from a place of respect.

That's what cultural exchange can look like—engaging with a culture as a respectful and humble guest, invitation only.

Don't overstay your welcome. Don't pretend to be a part of the household. Don't make yourself out to be an honored guest whom the householders should be grateful to entertain and educate for hours on end.

Don't ask a bunch of personal questions or make light of something that's clearly a sore spot. Just act like any polite house guest would by being attentive and knowing your boundaries.

If, instead, you try to approach another culture as a mooch, busy-body, or interloper, you will be shown the door. It's that simple.

Well, maybe not as simple when you move beyond the metaphor and into the real world. If you're from a so-called melting pot nation, you know what's it's like to be a perpetual couch surfer moving through the domains of many cultures.

Where Defining Cultural Appropriation Gets Messy

Is the Asian fusion takeout I order every week culturally appropriative? Even though I'm Black, is wearing dreadlocks appropriating forms of religious expression that really don't belong to me?

Is meditating cultural appropriation? Is Western yoga appropriation? Is eating a burrito, cosplaying, being truly fascinated by another culture, decorating with Shoji screens, or wearing a headscarf cultural appropriation?

There are so many things that have been chopped up, recolored, and tossed together to make up Western culture that even when we know things are appropriative in some way, we find them hard to let go of.

And then there are the things that have been freely shared by other cultures—Buddhism for example—that have been both respected and bastardized at different turns in the process of exchange.

At times, well-meaning people who struggle with their own appropriative behavior turn to textbooks, online comment boards, Google, and Tumblr ask boxes in search of a clear cut answer to the question, "Is this [insert pop culture thing, hairstyle, tattoo, or personal behavior here] cultural appropriation?"

That's a question we have to educate ourselves enough to, if not answer, think critically about.

We have a responsibility to listen to people of marginalized cultures, understand as much as possible the blatant and subtle ways in which their cultures have been appropriated and exploited, and educate ourselves enough to make informed choices when it comes to engaging with people of other cultures.

So if you're reading this and you're tired of people giving white women wearing bindis crap for appropriating because "freedom of speech," recognize that pointing out cultural appropriation is not personal.

This isn't a matter of telling people what to wear. It's a matter of telling people that they don't wear things in a vacuum and there are many social and historical implications to treating marginalized cultures like costumes.

It's also not a matter of ignoring "real" issues in favor of criticizing the missteps of a few hipsters, fashion magazines, or baseball teams.

Cultural appropriation is itself a real issue because it demonstrates the imbalance of power that still remains between cultures that have been colonized and the ex-colonizers.

Regardless, this is not an article asking you to over-analyze everything you do and wrack yourself with guilt.

Because honestly, no one cares about your guilt, no one cares about your hurt feelings, and no one cares about your clothes or hair when they're pointing out cultural appropriation.

When someone's behavior is labeled culturally appropriative, it's usually not about that specific person being horrible and evil.

It's about a centuries' old pattern of taking, stealing, exploiting, and misunderstanding the history and symbols that are meaningful to people of marginalized cultures.

The intentions of the inadvertent appropriator are irrelevant in this context.

Therefore, what this article is asking you to do is educate yourself, listen, and be open to reexamining the symbols you use without thinking, the cultures you engage with without understanding, and the historical and social climate we all need to be seeing.

EVALUATING THE AUTHOR'S ARGUMENTS:

In this viewpoint, Jarune Uwujaren says that respecting other cultures is the key to avoiding cultural appropriation. Other people may claim that you should avoid anything that could ever be considered cultural appropriation. And yet other people believe everyone should do what they want without worrying. Do you agree that there are times and places when it is acceptable to use aspects of another culture? Why or why not?

A Win for Free Speech Is Not a Win for Society

"There are sections of the public who will be attracted to a product or service precisely because of a controversial, unpleasant or even offensive message conveyed by the brand."

Enrico Bonadio

In the following viewpoint Enrico Bonadio argues that the ruling in a 2017 US legal case covering a trademark that was found to be offensive may allow other groups to trademark racist names. The case boils down to preserving free speech rights maintained by the First Amendment, but the author cautions against wholesale acceptance of offensive and disparaging language. He argues that it is important for governments to restrict these types of trademarks. Bonadio is Senior Lecturer at The City Law School of City, University of London.

AS YOU READ, CONSIDER THE FOLLOWING QUESTIONS:

1. How does the trademark ruling discussed change the future of what can be trademarked?
2. How might a company benefit from having a racist or otherwise offensive name?
3. How does the United States compare to other countries when it comes to denying registration for offensive terms?

You may not have heard of Asian-American dance-rock band, The Slants, but you may soon be very aware of a troubling precedent set after they won a contentious legal victory in the US Supreme Court.

Founder and bass player, Simon Tam, first tried to register the band's name as a trademark in 2011. It was refused because the brand was considered disparaging to people of Asian descent. Tam reckoned the derisive terms of "slants" or "slant eyes" were becoming anachronisms, ripe for re-purposing and a chance for Asian-Americans to have the power over how they were defined.

His success means that the band's brand is confirmed as registrable because it is protected by the first amendment to the US constitution. The Supreme Court opinion, in effect, says that the registration of a trademark cannot be banned on the grounds it conveys ideas that offend.

Race Is On

Good for Simon Tam, you might think. But the concern must be that this decision clears the way for the registration of many other names which are "scandalous, immoral or disparaging"—as the language of the law in question would have it. Registration of trademarks not only gives exclusive rights over brands, it encourages their owners to make investments around them and profit from the rights they have gained.

The case which most immediately springs to mind is that of the Washington Redskins. The American football team has been embroiled in a similar legal fight after the trademark office cancelled six registrations in 2014 under pressure from Native American groups, nearly 50 US senators, and the then-president Barack Obama.

The club's owner Dan Snyder was quick to realise the implications of the Slants ruling. "I am THRILLED," he said in a statement. "Hail to the Redskins!"

Those who praise this ruling may argue that trademark offices and judges should not be concerned with assessing whether a brand name is immoral, scandalous or offensive. Market forces alone—the argument goes—will be able to address such issues. If a brand is genuinely

Native Americans have lobbied sports teams such as the Washington Redskins to change their mascot.

upsetting or scandalous, consumers will vote with their wallets and push the brand out of the market.

On the Edge

That argument is flawed. I believe the Supreme Court decision is an encouragement to corporations and business people to register and use controversial and scandalous brands in the US in order to acquire market share. Clearly, there are sections of the public who will be attracted to a product or service precisely because of a controversial, unpleasant or even offensive message conveyed by the brand. That will apply particularly in industries such as fashion, where to be rude or "edgy" may pay off.

In a world where sections of the public complain loudly about the tyranny of political correctness, this ruling gives businesses leeway to loudly champion offensive or derogatory trademarks which mark that business out as a defender of those values and ideas. In other words, we will likely discover that offence sells—and may even become a driver of purchasing behaviour.

This shouldn't be a surprise. Brand identities are often chosen for their ability to shock customers, especially in the youth market, or at least to send ambiguous messages. The FCUK trademark adopted by the fashion company French Connection is a notable example. Beer company Brewdog has sought to emphasise its "edgy" credentials with brands such as Trashy Blonde.

Some of these attempts are clearly distasteful, especially when the aim is to capitalise on tragedies. One Malaysian company filed an application with the Australian trademark office to register the name MH17, just hours after the Malaysian Airlines flight had crashed into fields in eastern Ukraine, killing everyone on board. And dozens of people rushed to file trademark applications for exclusive rights over the brand "Je suis Charlie," just days after the terrorist attack at the Charlie Hebdo offices in Paris.

These examples highlight why it is important for governments to maintain the ability to police the registration of these types of trademarks. There needs to be a mechanism to stop registrations which go beyond what is broadly accepted as decent and which seek to win consumers' attention with brands which reinforce offensive views, or which cause needless distress to groups of people.

F**king Freezing

Countries other than US are quite strict when it comes to denying registration, and discouraging the use of offensive brands. In Europe for example trademark offices and judges have refused to protect racist terms such as "Paki" or words with sexually explicit or vulgar content, such as "Tiny Penis," "Screw you" and "F**king freezing."

Some of these decisions were based on the assumption that the refusal to register these words does not infringe free speech rights, a position diametrically opposed to the one taken by the US Supreme

Court in The Slants case. The ability to prohibit the registration of controversial brands is perceived in Europe as necessary to safeguard decency and morality in the course of trade and more importantly, protect ethnic and religious minorities as well as vulnerable people, including children.

Perhaps, if the US market eventually becomes flooded with openly racist and deliberately offensive brands, the Supreme Court will understand its mistake.

EVALUATING THE AUTHOR'S ARGUMENTS:

Consider this viewpoint in light of the previous viewpoints in this chapter. How does this trademark case relate to cultural appropriation? Should the band have the right to reclaim an offensive term? Or is this viewpoint's author correct in arguing that more good would be done by preventing groups from trademarking offensive terms? How should governments balance freedom of speech with protecting vulnerable groups?

Chapter 2

Are There Advantages to Cultural Appropriation?

Elvis Presley made a fortune popularizing a musical style borrowed from African American musicians in the South.

Cultural Appropriation? Get Over It

Michelle Malkin

> *"I'm just queasy and exhausted from trying to keep track of what we're supposed to wear and not wear."*

In the following viewpoint Michelle Malkin criticizes the idea of cultural appropriation. She suggests that there is a double standard for who is allowed to do what. She wonders why guests wearing costumes inspired by Catholic culture at the Met Gala were not considered offensive, if it is offensive to wear a sombrero on Cinco de Mayo. Malkin is an American conservative author and political commentator.

AS YOU READ, CONSIDER THE FOLLOWING QUESTIONS:
1. Who is complaining about the various behaviors listed? Are they people from within the culture or from outside of it?
2. What standard of behavior would you expect at an art museum's fund-raiser? Why?
3. How does the first sentence of the article set up your expectation of the author's viewpoint?

"The Left's Selective, Changing Rules on Cultural Appropriation," by Michelle Malkin, The Daily Signal, May 9, 2018. Reprinted by permission.

The impossibly fickle, selective, and whimsical rules of cultural appropriation are hard to keep straight.

(Oops! I said "straight." Apologies to whomever. Oops, can I say "whomever"? Zimever? Verselves? Gah.)

According to the white people who run the left-wing Southern Poverty Law Center, eating tacos, drinking tequila, and wearing sombreros on Cinco de Mayo "are textbook examples of cultural appropriation." Euro-privileged people at Gonzaga University similarly warned "non-Mexican individuals" on campus not to wear costumes insensitive to the "Latinx culture." No-nos included "serapes" and "fake mustaches."

An African-American writer at The Root, a website for "Black news, opinions, politics, and culture," counseled non-Mexican people on behalf of Mexican people to "cut it out with being a culturally appropriating jackass and leave the sombreros home."

According to the politically correct powers that be on Twitter, a white girl cannot wear a Chinese qipao dress to prom because Asian-Americans might be offended—even though actual Chinese people are not. The cultural contretemps was set off by a Chinese-American man, Jeremy Lam, who fumed, "My culture is NOT your g******ed prom dress"—while littering his own social media feed with ghetto slang ("N—- dayuum!") appropriated from rappers.

And a Korean-American restaurant owner came under fire recently for cheekily naming her business "Yellow Fever" (used to describe the condition of non-Asian males enamored of Asian females) to "embrace the term & reinterpret it positively."

To review the misappropriation mandates so far: Teenage white girls in Utah can't wear Chinese dresses to prom. Non-Mexicans can't wear sombreros on Cinco de Mayo. Wearing other groups' attire as costumes is insensitive. Re-appropriating phrases deemed inappropriate is inappropriate, even if done by a member of the aggrieved minority victimized by inappropriate appropriation. History shall not be trivialized. Identity must be respected.

So it is with extreme befuddlement and bewilderment that I sifted through pages and pages of photos from this week's Met Gala, whose theme was "Heavenly Bodies: Fashion and the Catholic Imagination."

Do we have to give up eating food that is not from our own culture? Should we boycott Americanized ethnic restaurants?

Pop diva Rihanna came dressed as a stiletto-heeled pope in pearls, crystals, and sky-high medieval headgear. (Will The Root writer scold her to cut it out with being a Catholic appropriating jackass and leave the bedazzled mitre at home?)

Nickelodeon alum Ariana Grande, draped in Vera Wang's cherub-adorned silk organza, chirped that she represented "the back wall of the Sistine Chapel" and felt "fairly important in this outfit, I have to say."

Entertainer Katy Perry, donning massive white feathered wings on her back that seem to have been borrowed from last year's Victoria's Secret runway, pronounced herself "angelic, celestial, ethereal."

FAST FACT

Cinco de Mayo is an annual holiday celebrated in parts of Mexico and the United States. In 1989, a beer importer introduced an ad campaign centered around the day, which led to the commercialization of the holiday in the United States.

Lana Del Rey, sprouting angel wings on top of her head, paired with Jared Leto decked out as Jesus in a gilt crown of thorns and powder blue Gucci suit.

Rosy-cheeked, mantilla-clad Kate Bosworth mimicked the Virgin Mary. Former Disney star Zendaya strutted the red carpet in Versace chain mail and Joan of Arc bangs. Nicki Minaj, last seen appropriating the Chinese martial arts video game cartoon character Chun Li (because that's OK), channeled the devil. And assorted supermodels and their arm candy escorts sported rosaries, halos, and veils like haute couture cosplay.

Now, this is the point at which I might cry out indignantly: My religion is not your costume! But the Vatican actually collaborated with the Met Gala on the event, donating prized vestments, cassocks, and other relics. No, I'm not offended. I'm just queasy and exhausted from trying to keep track of what we're supposed to wear and not wear, say and not say, eat or drink and not eat or drink, and who all is allowed to dictate what to whom and when.

"Piss Christ" is art. Muhammad cartoons are fatal blasphemy. Suburban girls in qipaos are human rights violators, but black female rappers and their fans in Chinese ox horn buns are cutting-edge. College kids in sombreros must be re-programmed, but Kim Kardashian parading like an oversized, gold-sequined chalice with crucifix stick-ons is high style.

The dizzying diktats of offense avoidance need to be burned like palm branches and tossed into an ash heap with campus offense-avoidance guidebooks. Can I get an amen on that? I say: Let me eat taco meat drenched in soy sauce with my chopsticks, drink a mango lassi while cooking latkes in my kimono, and be merry while making Spam musubi with my Catholic-Jewish-Ukrainian-Filipino-Chinese-Spanish kids.

Isn't that what celebrating diversity is all about?

Cultural Exchange Done Right

José Picardo

"Global awareness and international collaboration during the formative years results in more rounded individuals."

In the following viewpoint José Picardo argues that it is essential for young people to experience different countries and cultures. Understanding how others live expands our view of the world as well as helping us find our own place in the world. The author emphasizes the importance of schools supporting cultural exchange—both in the classrooms and on trips abroad, noting that social media can be a useful tool. Picardo is head of modern foreign languages at Nottingham High School in England.

AS YOU READ, CONSIDER THE FOLLOWING QUESTIONS:
1. What does the author say is a defining feature of people?
2. To what country did the author travel as a young person?
3. What benefits do social media bring to cultural exchange according to the viewpoint?

"Why students need a global awareness and understanding of other cultures," by José Picardo, Guardian News and Media Limited, September 25, 2012. Reprinted by permission.

As a languages teacher, it never ceases to astound me to think that the rasping, whistling and vibrating sounds emanating from our mouths and noses when you talk can be effortlessly decoded by our interlocutors as meaningful language, allowing us to communicate with one another in astonishing levels of complexity. Language is a defining feature of people.

In many western societies we might be tempted to assume that being able to speak and understand more than one language is the exception. However, it is estimated that between half and three quarters of the world's population is bilingual to some degree. That's more than four billion people who understand that with different languages come different ways to interpret the world.

Marcel Proust, the French novelist, observed that "the real voyage of discovery consists not in seeing new lands but in seeing with new eyes." He realised that by working with other people we learn about their cultures and become able to explore new ideas and prospects. Options that would not have occurred to us before stand out as obvious if we understand how other people experience the world. This is why, I believe, it is so important for students to have a deeper global awareness and understanding of other cultures.

In my own experience, leaving my small town in southern Spain to explore Italy for two weeks during my sixth form opened up a whole new world. As I found myself immersed in a different culture, it struck me that Italians, previously perceived by myself as peculiar beings, were in fact the norm in their context and that I was the stranger. Students nowadays are more likely to have travelled abroad by age of 16 and have easy access to a world of information through the internet. However, they still need to be guided through the process of discovery so that a deeper understanding of their own place in the word is developed.

This is why fostering global awareness and international collaboration in our classrooms are so beneficial to our students. Schools understand this and have traditionally encouraged the need to put learning into context. The history trip to Berlin, the French exchange, the cultural visit to Andalucía, pen pal writing schemes and foreign language assistants who bring a little bit of abroad into our classrooms are just a few of the many examples of contextualised learning that we provide our students. At my school we have three foreign

Visiting other parts of the world can expose teens to the best of cultural exchange.

language assistants and hold four foreign exchanges each year—in addition to a range of cultural trips abroad.

The moment in which a cohort of year 8 pupils land in Seville and realise that Spanish has a life beyond the textbook, the year 7s visiting Normandy and noticing that people behave and react in familiar ways but the small differences are what really matters. The awkward dinner conversations of foreign exchange students with their German host families, the sudden realisation that Dubai is such a long way away on so many different levels. These are character building experiences that bring out the best and worst in all of us and from which we learn so much.

However, in today's increasingly interconnected and globalised world, tradition is being supplemented by new and exciting ways to bring the world into our classrooms. Modern means of communication such as social networks and video conferencing can ensure that our students experience foreign cultures with unprecedented ease.

Class Twitter accounts link students in real time across the face of the planet with projects devised around common academic subjects and cross-cultural understanding. Skype allows us to converse face-to-face with people from other countries, allowing us to knock down classroom walls and hear it direct from the source. Google Maps lets our pupils take a walk down the streets of every major town and city in the world, allowing them to sight-see and get a sense of other cultures from the comfort of their own classroom. And blogs provide geographically distant schools with the means to partner together so that their pupils can interact in a safe virtual environment, contributing a valuable international dimension to peer assessment.

Both Britain—through the British Council—and the EU—through the Comenius and eTwinning programmes—are actively encouraging international partnerships between schools. These projects also promote the sharing of their resources so that, not only students, but also teachers can benefit from the exchange of practices, knowledge and expertise, with welcome positive implications for teacher training and professional development.

Global awareness and international collaboration during the formative years results in more rounded individuals, encouraging our pupils to see things from different perspectives and helping them to make informed decisions, acquiring transferable skills that will be useful to them and will remain with them for life. According to the Association of Graduate Recruiters companies cannot find enough applicants with the requisite skills to operate in an international market place, indicating that greater efforts by schools in fostering global awareness and international collaboration are needed to best prepare our students—and ourselves—for life in the 21st century.

EVALUATING THE AUTHOR'S ARGUMENTS:

How does viewpoint author José Picardo suggest that positive cultural exchange might prevent young people from engaging in cultural appropriation? Choose points from his argument and take them a step further to make your case.

The Censorship Imposed by Accusations of Cultural Appropriation Will Kill Art

"White free speech and white creative freedom have been founded on the constraint of others, and are not natural rights."

Mary Wakefield

In the following viewpoint Mary Wakefield discusses a painting at New York City's Whitney Museum that caused outrage. A white painter depicted a tragic moment in black history and was accused of benefiting from black suffering. The author claims that artistic creativity depends on artists having the freedom to tackle any subject. She blames young people for caring more about protests than about justice. She also accuses them of not thinking critically. Wakefield is commissioning editor of *The Spectator*, a weekly British magazine.

AS YOU READ, CONSIDER THE FOLLOWING QUESTIONS:

1. Why did critics believe a white artist should not have depicted the death of Emmett Till?
2. What point is Lionel Shriver trying to make about fiction?
3. Why is the author particularly criticizing young people?

It's usually best to ignore the indignant fury of the 21st-century young. We're used to them now, these snowflakes, posing as victims (though they're mostly middle-class), demanding "safe spaces," banning books and speakers. Best to rise above them, deadhead the camellias. Attention, especially from the press, acts on entitled millennials like water on gremlins—they start proliferating and develop a taste for blood.

But then sometimes they go too far.

Ten days ago, the Whitney museum, on the New York bank of the Hudson, opened its biennial exhibition of contemporary American art. It's an exciting show, full of vim and diversity. Half the artists represented are black, and the exhibition's stated aim is to confront racism and poverty in the States.

One of the white Whitney artists is a woman called Dana Schutz, and one of her paintings is of a famous photograph of a dead black boy, Emmett Till. Till was tortured and beaten to death in the mid-1950s by redneck bigots and Schutz's painting is called "Open Casket" because his brave mother chose to display his ruined face so that the world could see what had happened. The photograph, published in *Jet* magazine, helped change America. Schutz made the work, she says, because America still needs to change—as witnessed by the shooting of unarmed young black men by police.

So far, so unobjectionable—admirable even, right? Wrong. Since the Whitney opened its doors, there has been a non-stop wailing from twentysomethings on both sides of the Atlantic for the painting to be destroyed. Schutz is guilty of "cultural appropriation." Because she's white and a member of the oppressor class, she shouldn't have been allowed to depict black suffering. One young Brit, a writer called Hannah Black, wrote an open letter to the curators explaining that even if Schutz meant well, her painting is an abomination: "This painting should not be acceptable to anyone who cares or pretends to care about Black people because it is not acceptable for a white person to transmute Black suffering into profit and fun… The subject matter is not Schutz's; white free speech and white creative freedom have been founded on the constraint of others, and are not natural rights."

An event called "Kimono Wednesday" drew protesters to Boston's Museum of Fine Arts. The event invited visitors to try on a kimono in front of Monet's painting "La Japonaise."

An artist called Parker Bright has spent the week standing, arms folded, in front of the painting to hide it. He says it's "an injustice to the black community" which perpetuates "he same kind of violence that was enacted on Till."

The most worrying thing about the whole daft episode is not so much that the American press has taken it seriously, more the total disdain of these educated twentysomethings for reason. White free speech is not a natural right? Such confidence, such nonsense.

The gist of the protest is that Schutz, as a member of a fortunate class, should pipe down about the suffering of the less fortunate. But if the powerful can't champion underdogs, in the arts or in politics, how do these young warriors imagine anything will change? If, say, a white congressman were to speak out about the suffering of black men at the hands of cops, would that be cultural appropriation? If not, why not? Schutz was trying to change things too. Was it an appropriation of female suffering for John Stuart Mill to campaign for women's rights? I'm not sure there's ever been a more terrible own goal than this weird prohibition on good causes.

Because they don't believe in critical thought, because it's enough for these kids just to feel, they don't seem to realise that the world they want would be one without art. For one thing, they'll burn it; for another, the sort of censorship they suggest would kill creativity stone dead. No "Disasters of War" from Goya, no "Guernica" from rich, white Picasso.

FAST FACT

The Bell Curve: Intelligence and Class Structure in American Life is a 1994 book by Charles Alan Murray and Richard J. Herrnstein. In it they discuss human intelligence and racial differences in IQ scores.

A similar row trailed the writer Lionel Shriver last year after her speech at the Brisbane writers' festival in which she attacked the notion of "cultural appropriation" in literature. Shriver said: "The ultimate endpoint of keeping our mitts off experience that doesn't belong to us is that there is no fiction. Someone like me only permits herself to write from the perspective of a straight white female born in North Carolina, closing on 60, able-bodied but with bad knees, skint for years but finally able to buy the odd new shirt. All that's left is memoir."

And who do these righteous muppets think should decide on culturally appropriate subjects for writers and artists? Do they imagine a licensing body, an arm of government going from studio to studio checking for privilege? The truth is, they don't imagine anything. They just don't do sustained thought. For them, it's enough to harangue, and to signal lofty indifference to criticism on Twitter: "Wow. Just wow."

If the most worrying thing is the lack of logic, the saddest thing about the Schutz affair is the lack of empathy. Parker Bright compares Dana Schutz to the vicious, racist thugs who tortured Emmett Till to death. What about her feelings? A Twitter kid posted a photo of Schutz with the words "Burn this s***, b***" scrawled across it in red like a death threat.

Unchecked by reason, therefore unworried by hypocrisy, snowflakes creep closer and closer towards actual violence. The week before the Whitney show opened, students at Middlebury College in Vermont turned out to protest against a talk by Charles Murray, author of *The Bell Curve*. Having long ago decided that free speech is hurtful and unnecessary, they crowded around Murray chanting "Who is the enemy? White supremacy!" and "Anti-black, anti-gay, go away!" There's no evidence that Murray is anti-gay or racist, but if you self-define as a victim, you can be as aggressive and offensive as you like.

They jumped on his car, rocking and pounding it. Unable to get at Murray, one male demonstrator grabbed a female professor by the hair and twisted her head. She ended up in hospital. But that's not cultural appropriation, so who cares?

EVALUATING THE AUTHOR'S ARGUMENTS:

Viewpoint author Mary Wakefield begins by criticizing young people. Did this affect the way you read the piece? If so, how so? What does this technique suggest about her intended audience? Try re-reading the article with a focus on looking past the emotional language at the points the author makes. Does your reaction change any?

Fitting In Is Merely Survival

Rachel Kuo

"Things from my culture that were seen as bizarre and weird when I was growing up are now being viewed as 'trendy.'"

In the following viewpoint Rachel Kuo debates whether people of color can appropriate white culture. She states that marginalized people cannot appropriate from the dominant culture. It is not appropriation when people copy the culture that is treated as normal, she says. In fact, behaving as "normal" by the standards of the dominant culture can be necessary. It may be the only way that people can get jobs, navigate society, and be perceived as professional. Rachel Kuo studies racial justice and digital media activism in the doctoral program in Media, Culture, and Communications at New York University.

AS YOU READ, CONSIDER THE FOLLOWING QUESTIONS:
1. What does the author mean by "Appropriation is ultimately about power"?
2. What is meant by the "dominant culture"?
3. What is assimilation?

"5 Reasons Why People of Color Cannot Appropriate White Culture in the US," by Rachel Kuo, Everyday Feminism, February 28, 2016. Reprinted by permission.

B
ut you speak English!" "You eat hamburgers and pizza." "You use forks!" "You wear jeans." "Your name, Rachel, appropriates from White people!"

So, basically, living in the United States, if I don't only do things stereotypically marked as "Asian," I'm appropriating from White culture? And, if I do whatever non-Asian folks imagine "being Asian" looks like, I'm told, "Go back to China?"

My family isn't from there by the way.

There's been a lot of back and forth lately in discussions of appropriation that question the incorporation of "White culture" into people of color's day to day lives.

When White folks claim that people of color are appropriating their culture, there is a misunderstanding of what is actually meant by appropriation. Saying, "Hey! It's appropriation when Asians speak English!" or "If we can't wear dreads, then black folks can't straighten their hair" is an inaccurate oversimplification of cultural appropriation.

They ask, "So you borrow from our culture, but we can't take from yours?"

Not only does this question re-center a conversation about the appropriation of marginalized communities' cultures around the feelings and needs of White people, but cultural appropriation cannot be simplified to just the act of experiencing another culture—whether that's traveling, eating food, or appreciating art.

When thinking about cultural appropriation, one of the first things that came to mind for me were how things from my culture that were seen as bizarre and weird when I was growing up are now being viewed as "trendy."

Like how the herbal soups my mom made for when I was sick was seen as strange-smelling with weird little orange things, but now goji berries are a hot superfood.

But, cultural appropriation is more complicated than people outside of my descent starting to incorporate my culture into their day-to-day lives.

We need to think about how power and privilege work in discussions of cultural appropriation.

If a country like the United States is considered a melting pot, how can its citizens know what is appropriation and what is part of the country's culture?

Appropriation is ultimately about power. Cultural appropriation refers to a specific power dynamic where members of a dominant culture take elements from a culture of people that they continue to systematically oppress.

We have think about what is actually being communicated when aspects of culture are taken in piecemeal.

A group whose culture has been minimized, disenfranchised, and marginalized can't appropriate from a culture who has the power to demean and disadvantage other cultures.

So, this is not a conversation about when people of color appropriate from other communities of color—that's a different discussion all together. Yes, it is possible for people of color to appropriate other cultures, but in the United States, it is not possible for people of color to appropriate culture from White folks.

There's no such thing as "reverse" cultural appropriation and here's why:

1. "Dominant Culture" or "White Culture" Defines Everyone Else's Reality

Try this: Think about how many famous white visual artists you can name. How many artists of color can you think of?

Whether or not you know much about art or whose work is hanging up in museums right now, I'm betting there's a big chance you can name way more white artists than people of color.

These are issues of access, opportunity, and representation that all manifest in one clear message about whose culture is worth knowing, worth sharing widely, and worth valuing.

Dominant culture—so in the case of the US, White culture—is the one that is perceived as normal, as part of the status quo. It's an ever present part of everyone's reality, no matter their background.

In fact, it's considered so normal, that it's hard to name precisely what White culture specifically is. We are socialized to live it, believe in it, and accept it. It's internalized within us.

In the US, often when people refer to Americans or "American culture," they're also referring specifically to Whiteness. All other cultural backgrounds get a qualifier, such as Asian Americans, Black Americans, Latinx Americans.

I grew up in a predominantly white and middle class suburb in the Midwest and later went to college in mid-Missouri. Whiteness was not only the norm, but also constantly reinforced as the cultural standard.

This was evident in the racial identities of teachers and professors in charge of the classroom. It was evident the "canonical" books we were assigned in class like *Catcher in the Rye* and *The Great Gatsby* and the history we learned that focused solely on Western civilization including the "discovery" of America.

Different processes, including colonization, turned different groups of European immigrants into the racially elite White community. White culture is the dominant power because it controls everyone's reality through controlling things like history, language, and culture.

"Reverse" cultural appropriation isn't possible, because our culture supports and enforces Whiteness as the norm.

When a racial group has decided that their culture and lifestyle is the best and only option for everyone else, then it's not appropriation when others emulate them.

I have to partake in White culture just from the reality of existing in this current moment in time—I'm not "borrowing" from it simply for my own whimsical pleasures whenever it suits me.

2. Cultural Appropriation Isn't Just About Borrowing Culture

Often, claims of "reverse" appropriation are the dominant group's knee jerk reaction to being told something is off-limits. Conversations about what is or isn't cultural appropriation often end up being a tired discussion about what is or isn't oversensitive "policing" and forcing people to stay in their own "cultural lane."

I've also heard people say things like, "So, I'm White, does this mean I don't get to eat dim sum? You're expecting me to only eat hamburgers my whole life?" Or, "I'm White, does this mean I can't wear a kimono that I bought in a department store during my trip to Japan?"

The complex nuances of what's actually at play totally get lost.

Participation and appropriation are totally different things. Cultural appropriation is not just about who does or doesn't get to participate in, wear, or try other cultures. So, then, the "if I don't get to wear my hair in cornrows, then you don't get to have bangs" argument doesn't really make sense.

The problem with appropriation isn't that people are incorporating aspects of other cultures into their everyday life—from what they wear, what they eat, and what they consume.

Rather, its the complete erasure of historical context and the total disregard of oppression experienced and endured throughout history.

For example, someone who wears Native headdress or a bindi because it's now cute and fashionable is taking from another culture's spiritual and/or cultural practices but not understanding the value and importance.

We need to be more mindful of how cultures and communities get caricaturized and reduced into a singular costume or artifact.

3. There's a Huge Difference Between Assimilation and Appropriation

Assimilation is when a marginalized group has to take on aspects from the dominant culture for survival.

When my parents first immigrated to the US from Taiwan, they had to learn English and also understand how to navigate institutions and policies to figure out how to get jobs and make an income here. They learned to adopt different behaviors, including American-based cultural traditions, just by living here.

When other groups adopt behaviors that have been coded as White, or as "normal," in order to gain wealth, employment, or other benefits, that's not appropriation—that's trying to survive.

For example, wearing a suit or other "business" attire coded as White in order to appear more professional reinforces pressures to conform with White culture.

Another example of this comes out of discussions of hair and beauty politics. Maisha Z. Johnson talks about how when Black women straighten their hair, it's often a matter of survival to be treated with more respect and to be perceived as more "professional."

The hair of the dominant group of people, White people, and the way they are easily able to cut and style that hair, becomes seen as not only normal, but professionally and socially acceptable. Black hair in its natural state is seen as messy and inferior.

When Beyonce wore a blond wig with side-swept bangs, some folks accused her of appropriating White culture and that it was a double standard to accuse Kylie Jenner of appropriation for wearing cornrows but not Beyonce for rocking the wig and bangs.

Now, while people might argue that Beyonce is so famous that there's just no way she can experience oppression, it falsely assumes that having privilege automatically erases all other experiences of oppression.

Any conversation about hair and appropriation can't be reduced down to who gets to wear what hairstyle without a closer examination of the specific power dynamics in racialized beauty politics.

4. Colonization Established the Dominance of White Culture

We also continue to live with the legacies of colonialism that impact our everyday consumption, from shopping for clothes and buying food.

Places that have been colonized, including the United States, forced people in those places to take on the culture of the colonizer by forcibly removing other aspects of culture.

Forced assimilation, emphasis on force, violently removes other cultures.

Groups, such as Indigenous nations, were forced to assimilate, as government policies pushed the removal of language and other traditions.

When Europeans stole people from different parts of Africa to be used as slaves, they tried to strip away any cultural identity. In the US and Canada, Indigenous children were separated from their families to attend boarding schools where they were forced to speak English and adopt Western culture.

"Civilization" disguised as education was a systematic way White culture became dominant.

As communities have worked to resist this systematic removal and hold on to their cultural practice, it's then effed up when other people then use these cultural artifacts and symbols out of context, just for their own fleeting fun and fashion.

5. White Folks Aren't Oppressed By Their Racial/Ethnic Culture

Yes, White people in the US have their own ethnic histories full of struggle and hardship as well as cultural traditions that they strongly affiliate with, celebrate, and are proud of.

But because White people are not oppressed racially in the United States or in other Western countries, they are not oppressed by the ways racism extends itself socially, economically, and culturally.

White people are not systematically discriminated against when they practice, wear, or display their cultural traditions.

For example, let's talk about St. Patrick's Day, which has often been discussed as a religious holiday that has been stripped of cultural meaning and turned into an excuse for drunken revelry.

Although many immigrants, like Irish, Italian, and Polish immigrants, were oppressed and treated as "non-White" during their arrival in the early 1800s, they gradually were able to become accepted as White as immigration policies determined who was "American" was based on who looked American.

Thus, Irish Americans are no longer systematically disenfranchised for showing off their cultural roots.

I can also guarantee that the reception of a large group of White people participating in drunk public spectacle is quite different than the reception of a group of people of color in drunken spectacle or even, a group of people of color having fun—please refer to the Sistahs of Reading Edge Book Club being kicked off a wine tour for laughing too loudly while Black.

However, cultural and spiritual garments and customs when worn, used, or done by people of color can turn them into racialized targets. For example, a non-White person who wears a hijab or other marker of Muslim identity (or are even perceived as Muslim) might encounter Islamophobia.

Racial hierarchies that favor Whiteness and that endorse and protect White culture are created and imposed by White people.

So, it's not right if a group wants to be able to take cultural elements from other racial group but also maintain hierarchies that systematically denies access benefits to those same people they're "borrowing" from.

Plus, cultures from communities of color end up appropriated into White culture. Like how pumpkin spice, which includes spices that belonged to people of color and Indigenous people, became something associated with Whiteness.

Or how wearing yoga pants is something that is now generalized to be associated with upper class White women. Or rock and roll, which was hugely influenced by a Black woman, Rosetta Tharpe.

When cultures are exchanged, appreciated, and acknowledged in respectful, accountable ways, there can be so much creative and exciting possibilities for cultural production.

However, you can't want to disenfranchise other cultures, take elements from those cultures that seem fun and interesting, and then also blame other cultures for wanting to be "like you" in order to access the same things you can access.

EVALUATING THE AUTHOR'S ARGUMENTS:

Viewpoint author Rachel Kuo insists that when people of color adopt white cultural practices, it is not cultural appropriation. Do you agree with her logic? Why or why not? How do the opinions in previous viewpoints support or challenge these views?

Cultural Appropriation Is Love

T. J. Brown

"Who are you to tell someone that they aren't allowed to express their love for another culture?"

In the following viewpoint T. J. Brown sings the praises of cultural appropriation—not because it denigrates others but because it is a love letter to them. The author maintains that appreciation of other cultures has been stifled in recent times because we have been made to feel uncomfortable or racist for wanting to emulate people who are unlike ourselves. He blames this development on petty fights between the political left and right, which ultimately have created an environment in which the focus is on appropriation rather than appreciation and reverence. T. J. Brown lives in Atlanta and hosts a YouTube channel.

AS YOU READ, CONSIDER THE FOLLOWING QUESTIONS:
1. Why is the author thrilled to see Asian kids dressing up as the Jackson 5?
2. How have the far left and the alt-right become enablers of each other according to the viewpoint?
3. How do charges of cultural appropriation inhibit creativity and freedom according to the author?

I 've never been able to get into the Halloween spirit. Maybe that's because most of my childhood's trick-or-treating consisted of candy corn. But as I've grown, I've gained a new appreciation for this holiday. It's an exhibition and embrace of cultural diversity through costumes and tog.

Honoring the Other

When I see a beautiful Caucasian woman dressing up as a Salsa Dancer, or a group of Asian college students dressed as the Jackson Five, it resonates with me in a very positive way. The Salsa Dancer dressed as such because she sees the beauty of the culture, attire, and people that are associated. She adores this culture so much that she's willing to spend her own money to embody it for a single night. The Asian kids dressing up as the Jackson Five clearly have not only knowledge of the legendary African-American pop sensation, but have also been impacted by the cultural talents they delivered to the market.

This is why I see Cultural Appropriation as a gesture of love within humanity. It's a refreshing deviation from conventional US ethnocentric patriotism and isolation. I'm thrilled to see people dressing up as diverse identities from around the globe, and not just wearing American Flag trucker hats and Confederate bikinis.

As our culture becomes more and more politically correct and censorious of "offensive" displays of cultural mimicry, diversity has become less about expressions of humanistic cooperation, and more about competitive oppression.

In PC parlance, that Salsa Dancer costume is actually insensitive to the economic suffering of Hispanic women who had to subject themselves to patriarchal theater. That Jackson Five getup ignores the capitalist exploitation by the music industry of black artists during the American Civil Rights movement. This is the narrative you will commonly hear pushed on many progressive university campuses and blog sites.

Some find this to be annoying, but I'd actually go as far as to call it outright insulting and abusive. Who are you to tell someone that they aren't allowed to express their love for another culture because you arbitrarily hold exclusive claim to it? Who are you to

Is it offensive when tourists bring home souvenirs from their travels?

micromanage identity and dictate what types of multiculturalism is tolerable and intolerable?

In the attempt made by progressives to socially abolish what they rule as problematic cultural appropriation, the actual effect is to make harmonious ethnic relations less likely to occur.

That Which Separates Us

Once a white man dressing up as an Arabian Sheik or a black man dressing up as an Irish bagpiper was met with excitement and interest. Now there exists a mob to ridicule them into hiding for being racist bigots. Basically they are saying to these men, "You are different and should stick to your own kind."

How is that helpful to advancing equality or association? Now these two men are intellectually isolated, likely fostering resentment for diversity. This is dangerous for everyone, especially cultural minorities.

The far left and the Alt-Right have become enablers of each other. While the Alt-Right shames whites for abandoning their heritage and culture and demands that non-whites appropriate European culture, the far left shames whites (primarily) for embracing and adopting cultural differences and contrasts and demands they NOT appropriate.

Neither side wants to break down polarities; neither side wants a free and natural marketplace of voluntary inclusivity and association. I oppose both these factions, which is why I endorse more cultural appropriation not only on Halloween, but every day.

A world without cultural appropriation is a world without learning, emulation, aspiration, celebration, and progress. It is a frozen and dull world of isolation and insularity.

You don't have to be an assimilative glob of clay to be properly molded by the right or a self-hating ally of the left. Culture is spontaneous, and your expression of it should be as well. So to the white girls, wear box braids if you want. To the black girls, don't let haters stop you from rocking that blonde relaxer. Dress up as cowboys and Indians, black and white celebrities.

If you're trans and want to dress as a cis person or visa-versa, do it. Your life is not present to be ordered and manipulated by central planners, governments, fascists, or social justice warriors. Your life is present to pursue your own self-interests and to find what makes you happy. Accusations of degeneracy or racism be damned.

EVALUATING THE AUTHOR'S ARGUMENTS:

Viewpoint author T. J. Brown uses the example of Halloween costumes to urge people to dress up in whatever way they want. How does his viewpoint differ from the viewpoint in the previous chapter that also used Halloween as a launching point to make an argument?

Chapter 3

Who Is Harmed by Cultural Appropriation and How?

A young girl dresses as Princess Jasmine in the Magic Kingdom.

Racist Stereotypes Cause More Racism

Justin Angle

"Studies have shown how stereotypes of any kind— even positive ones—carry consequences. "

In the following viewpoint Justin Angle explores how racial stereotypes affect people. He led academic research that studied how people reacted to sports mascots. The study showed people sports mascots based on Native Americans. Seeing these Native American stereotypes caused viewers to feel that Native Americans were more warlike. This could affect how Native Americans are treated in society. It could even mean they are more often convicted of crimes and given harsher sentences. A real-world experiment confirmed the findings. Justin Angle is Assistant Professor of Marketing at the University of Montana.

AS YOU READ, CONSIDER THE FOLLOWING QUESTIONS:
1. What is implicit bias?
2. How does implicit bias affect people's decision making?
3. How can a positive stereotype hurt people?

For years, many have said that sports teams with Native American mascots—the Cleveland Indians, Chicago Blackhawks and Florida State Seminoles, to name a few—perpetuate stereotypes against Native people. Others have argued that these mascots are harmless; if anything, they symbolize reverence and respect, while honoring the history of Native Americans.

At the epicenter of the debate have been the Washington Redskins, a football team worth nearly US$3 billion. But as the Redskins kicked off their season on Sept. 12, there was hardly a mention of the name controversy that has, in recent years, elicited boycotts, lawsuits and protests.

Perhaps it's due to the Washington Post survey from last spring finding that 90 percent of the Native Americans polled weren't offended by the Redskins name. Since then, defenders of the name—including team owner Daniel Snyder—have considered the controversy over and done with. The "sticks and stones" argument suggested by the poll makes complete sense from a self-preservation standpoint; after all, Native Americans have had to persevere through worse offenses than mascots.

But that stance ignores the dangerous possibility that such ethnic names and imagery affect how other people view Native Americans—possibly in subtle and damaging ways.

Our research has shown that incidental exposure to Native American sports mascots can reinforce stereotypes in people. Perhaps more disturbingly, people aren't even aware that this subtle reinforcement is taking place.

How a Name Strengthens a Bias

In our lab, we showed participants an unfamiliar mascot; some were shown a Native American image, while others were shown an image of an animal. We then measured how strongly all participants associated Native Americans with "warlike," a stereotype leveraged by many sports teams that use Native mascots ("Braves," "Warriors"). When asked directly, participants, regardless of the mascot they saw, reported no differences in how warlike they thought Native Americans were.

But when participants completed an indirect—or implicit—stereotype measure, those who'd viewed the Native American

Exposure to Native American sports mascots can reinforce harmful stereotypes.

mascot were more likely to associate warlike qualities with Native Americans.

This difference in results represents something called implicit bias, which often takes place when asking people about socially sensitive subjects such as race or gender. Our participants were either unwilling to admit or unaware of the mascot's influence on their views of Native Americans; their bias was implicit, either hidden or incognizant.

Implicit bias can influence decisions ranging from hiring practices to jury preferences and criminal sentencing. And it's all the more pernicious because the people making these biased decisions are unlikely to be aware that they're doing so.

Interestingly, the liberal participants in our studies were more affected by Native American mascots than were their conservative peers.

Because liberals often think of themselves as being less susceptible to racial bias, this might seem counterintuitive. But liberals also have been shown to have more malleable worldviews and be more open to new information. And in our study, we found a stereotypical mascot

FAST FACT

Implicit bias refers to attitudes that affect our understanding, decisions, and actions in an unconscious manner. The news, social media, marketing, and life experiences can all affect implicit bias.

could significantly degrade liberals' attitudes toward Native Americans.

Some Mascots More Damaging Than Others

These lab results prompted us to try to replicate our findings in a real world setting. If the media market you live in determines how often you're exposed to a Native American sports mascot, we would expect to see differences in attitudes toward Native Americans between people who live in cities with Native American-themed sports franchises and people who don't. Indeed, our results showed that people living in cities with Native American mascots were more likely to think of Native Americans as warlike.

We decided to focus on the Cleveland and Atlanta media markets because the Native American mascots of their baseball teams—the Indians and the Braves—were considered the most and least offensive examples, respectively, according to a pre-experiment survey. (Detroit, home of the Tigers, and Miami, which houses the Marlins, were used as control cities.)

Using the same implicit measures as our earlier study, residents of Cleveland were more likely to associate Native Americans with warlike traits than residents of Atlanta, Detroit and Miami.

In other words, the more offensive the mascot, the greater the effect.

And just like in our lab, liberal participants were particularly sensitive to the influence of the Native American mascot. The study represents perhaps the first real-world demonstration of the adverse effects of incidental exposure to Native American sports mascots in the general population.

The Perils of Stereotypes

Some might wonder what the problem is with being seen as warlike. After all, isn't that associated with bravery and toughness?

But studies have shown how stereotypes of any kind—even positive ones—carry consequences. They can lead to performance anxiety, as Sapna Cheryan and her colleagues found when looking at stereotypes concerning Asian Americans' math ability. Subsequent studies have shown how experiencing a positive stereotype can make people expect future prejudicial treatment.

Despite these findings, defenders of Native American mascots continue to argue that the mascots honor Native Americans and improve perceptions of Native people.

Furthermore, stereotypical representations of minority groups aren't just relegated to Native American team mascots.

Many prominent brands, such as Aunt Jemimah, Uncle Ben's and Land-O-Lakes Butter, actively promote certain stereotypes. And as our study showed, these representations can change how we think about the actual members of those groups—often without us even knowing it.

So when it comes to the Washington Redskins—despite the results of the spring poll—the evidence is clear: The presence of the name subconsciously causes people to stereotype Native Americans. Even President Obama has weighed in, recommending a new name.

He's right. It's high time for change.

EVALUATING THE AUTHOR'S ARGUMENTS:

In this viewpoint, Justin Angle argues that stereotypes used in marketing can cause harm. Are you convinced that sports teams and companies should change their mascots, names, and marketing efforts? Why or why not? What are some possible challenges and side effects of changes such as these?

Viewpoint 2

Understand History to Do Better in the Future

Olufunmilayo Arewa

"In some instances, a line is crossed and cultural borrowing can become exploitative."

In the following viewpoint Olufunmilayo Arewa focuses on the appropriation of African cultural creations. She notes that Africa has a history of being invaded by colonial powers. These powers not only took over countries and killed people but they also seized cultural property and sold it for profit. The author suggests that examining the past can give guidance for the future. Borrowing ideas and cultural expressions should acknowledge the source and compensate the original creators, she feels. This is especially important when the groups are not equal in power. Olufunmilayo Arewa is Professor of Law at the University of California, Irvine. Her research centers around intellectual property and business, with a primary focus on copyright and music.

1. How are the Benin Bronzes an example of historical cultural appropriation?
2. How is the song "The Lion Sleeps Tonight" a more recent historical example of cultural appropriation?
3. Why is the fairytale Cinderella an example of how cultures borrow and mix ideas?

The idea of "cultural appropriation" has recently entered mainstream debates about the ways in which African cultural creations are used, borrowed and imitated by others. In fashion, art, music and beyond, some people now argue that certain African cultural symbols and products are off-limits to non-Africans.

In March 2016, an African-American woman at San Francisco State University confronted a white student. She said he should cut his hair because dreadlocks belong to black culture. The incident went viral. Within a month, a YouTube video of the encounter had been watched more than 3.7 million times.

An online debate also erupted about whether it was appropriate for Canadian singer Justin Bieber to wear dreadlocks.

Debates about appropriation aren't always limited to cross-racial borrowing. An online discussion about African-American appropriation of African cultural symbols also went viral. It began with journalist Zipporah Gene asking black Americans to stop appropriating African clothing and tribal marks. She argued this indicated "ignorance and cultural insensitivity."

In these debates, the label of cultural appropriation is broadly applied to borrowing that is in some way inappropriate, unauthorised or undesirable. My argument is that borrowing may become appropriation when it reinforces historically exploitative relationships or deprives African countries of opportunities to control or benefit from their cultural material.

FAST FACT

Benin is a nation in west Africa that achieved independence from France in 1960.

A History of Extraction

During colonialism, colonial powers not only extracted natural resources but also cultural booty.

The contemporary cultural appropriation debate reflects a justified sensitivity about this historical legacy of extraction, evidence of which can be found in various museums outside of Africa.

The theft of the renowned Benin Bronzes is just one example of this cultural looting. These artifacts were seized by the British in 1897 during a punitive military expedition against the Kingdom of Benin. British soldiers invaded, looted, and ransacked Benin, setting buildings on fire and killing many people. They then deposed, shackled and exiled the Oba (king). This ultimately spelled the end of the independent Kingdom of Benin.

The punitive force looted an estimated 3,000 bronzes, ivory-works, carved tusks and oak chests. Benin's cultural heritage was then sold in the private European art market to offset the cost of the expedition. Today the Benin Bronzes can be found in museums and collections worldwide. And, in 1990, one single Benin head was sold for US$2.3 million by a London-based auction house.

In 2010, a looted Benin mask with an estimated value of £4.5 million was withdrawn from sale by Sotheby's auction house following protests concerning the sale. The mask was due to be sold by descendants of a participant in the punitive expedition.

In contrast, the descendant of one participant in the looting of Benin has returned looted artwork.

This colonial booty was taken without permission or compensation. Some people argue a similar dynamic exists in contemporary use of African cultural symbols, creations and products.

Cultural Fluidity

Accusations of cultural appropriation raise important and complex questions about the nature of culture. The reality of human experience is that borrowing and cultural mixture are widespread. This is

The Benin Bronzes, taken from Africa in the nineteenth century, have been displayed in the British Museum.

evident in language, religion, agriculture, folklore, food and other cultural elements.

The fairy tale Cinderella provides a good example. Versions of the story can be traced back to the Far East, Near East, Eastern Europe, Southern Europe and Northern Europe. By the mid-20th century, the Cinderella story could be found in India, North Africa, North America, the Western Sudan, Madagascar, Mauritius, the Philippines and Indonesia.

Cultural boundaries are fluid and shifting. Cultural systems may be significantly transformed by different forces and influences. This means that incomplete discussions of appropriation may fail to account for borrowing, diffusion, collaboration and other factors that lead to cultural material being shared.

Discussions of appropriation may also take insufficient account of the importance and benefits of borrowing. Borrowing has led to the international spread of denim, mathematics and even democracy.

When Borrowing Becomes Appropriation

In some instances, a line is crossed and cultural borrowing can become exploitative. Crossing this line may turn acts of borrowing into cultural appropriation.

Context, particularly as it relates to power relationships, is a key factor in distinguishing borrowing from exploitative cultural appropriation.

For example, cultural borrowing from Africa must be considered in the context of historical power asymmetries between Africa and the rest of the world. This is particularly the case with European powers, which developed trading relationships and spheres of influence in Africa.

These later formed the basis for colonial territories. Relationships between African countries and the colonial powers were often extractive and included varied forms of cultural imperialism.

Examining past instances of borrowing can give guidance for future models. Continuing discussions and a lawsuit about the song "The Lion Sleeps Tonight" are noteworthy. This discussion draws attention to the Zulu musician Solomon Linda, who received little compensation for his song Mbube, recorded in 1939. Linda's song became "The Lion Sleeps Tonight," a global pop classic that has generated substantial money for others.

When patterns of borrowing fail to acknowledge their sources and compensate them, they can be categorized as cultural appropriation. This is particularly the case when cultural flows reflect, reinforce or magnify inequalities. Even in instances where sources receive compensation, later compensation does not always redress past inequities.

The Linda family did eventually receive compensation after filing suit. When Linda died in 1962, his widow could not afford to purchase a gravestone. His daughter died of AIDS-related illness in 2001 because she was unable to afford antiretroviral medication.

How to Block Exploitative Practices

Understanding the context of borrowing is important for preventing exploitative cultural appropriation. An understanding of both borrowing and appropriation should be incorporated into legal, business and other institutional frameworks.

In fields such as intellectual property law, greater recognition of the power structures underlying borrowing in different contexts is important.

This can be an important starting point for blocking future exploitative cultural flows. And it can help prevent extraction of more cultural booty.

EVALUATING THE AUTHOR'S ARGUMENTS:

In this viewpoint Olufunmilayo Arewa compares current uses of African culture to the theft of African cultural items in the past. Do you agree with her comparisons? In what ways might understanding the past help us make better decisions in the present?

Fashion Trends Can Show a Disrespect for Culture

"Why are they being exotic and creative, while I am being ridiculed for embracing an aspect of my culture?"

Fatima Farha

In the following viewpoint Fatima Farha explores the history of the bindi. She criticizes people who wear a bindi as a fashion trend, and not because they understand and share the cultural history. She notes that Westerners criticize Hindu women who wear a bindi. Yet when Westerners wear the bindi themselves, it is seen as an exotic and trendy fashion. Fatima Farha wrote this article for a student-run news website at Niles West High School in Skokie, Illinois, when she was a student.

AS YOU READ, CONSIDER THE FOLLOWING QUESTIONS:
1. What is the cultural significance of the bindi?
2. How do people treat South Asian women who wear the bindi, according to the author?
3. How do people treat Western women differently when they wear the bindi, according to the author?

Fashion trends are ongoing. One day it'll be something, and the next day it will be something else, and that is completely fine. There is nothing wrong with fashion, and there is nothing wrong with the trends that people set. However, there is a limit, a limit that requires respecting people's cultures, heritage, traditions, and most importantly, what can be fashion and what can't.

In the past couple of months, I have seen a rising fashion trend of the bindi, a gem worn on the forehead between the eyebrows. On fashion websites, I've seen these bindis sold as sticky gems that can just be stuck to the forehead, sold in different shapes and colors, in different designs.

The bindis have grown prominence and many girls have started wearing them. Just last weekend, Selena Gomez decided to sport a huge bindi during her performance at the MTV Movie Awards for her new single, "Come and Get It."

The girls who wear it call the bindi "exotic" and find it very cool because it is a part of the Indian culture, and they think it's pretty. The funny part is, none of the girls who actually wear the bindi in terms of this fashion trend are Indian. Or even close to South Asians.

So where did this "exotic" bindi come from? The bindi is a forehead decoration worn by women in South Asia. It comes from the Hindu culture and religion, so the majority of the women who wear it are South Asian Hindus.

The bindi can symbolize many aspects of the Hindu culture, but from the beginning it has always been a red dot worn on the forehead, most commonly to represent a married woman. The bindi is also said to be the third eye in Hindu religion, and it can be used to ward off bad luck. The women who wear it in India wear it with some representation of their own culture, whether it's because they're married, or if they have another cultural tie to it.

As times progressed, the bindi acquired more designs, and today there are many different kinds of bindis that women wear, with different colors and designs to match their daily outfits, or fancy ones for their fancy dresses. However, at the end of the day, it is a part of their culture, and they wear it with that significance.

The women who wear it today, in the Western countries, are not wearing it with that culture in mind. Instead, they wear it because it

Fashion designers routinely release collections inspired by "exotic" cultures and benefit financially from this appropriation.

looks exotic and they try to be trendy, but do they even know what the cultural significance is?

A bindi has a lot of significance to the women who wear it in South Asia, and by not keeping that in mind, the women who wear it here and who are not from South Asia are disrespecting it to a very high degree. They are culturally appropriating the bindi.

Cultural appropriation is a term that defines the adoption of a minority's culture by the dominant culture. The dominant culture takes the minority's culture, or a part of it, and makes it seem menial, without any of the significance that it was supposed to have.

Even though many people think that adopting aspects of another culture can be thought of as "sharing," that doesn't justify not respecting what that object means in the actual culture it was stolen from. And the

reason it is so frustrating is because the dominant culture does not have to suffer any racism because of it.

When Hindu women in the United States wear the bindi, people love to make fun of them. I have heard a countless number of jokes about the bindi. If you watch "Family Guy," and even if you don't, you've probably seen the scene where Peter Griffin asks his neighbor whether he uses the "red button" on his wife's forehead as a remote control to shut her up. When people in the Western countries, such as America, see an actual Indian woman wearing the bindi, she is coined as a fob, a backwards and old-fashioned person who does not know how to embrace the American culture.

But somehow, when the dominant culture in America decides to adopt this "trend," they are called exotic and beautiful. The stigma that the South Asian women face because of their cultural identity choices is very offensive, and it hurts more when people who aren't even from this culture wear it and don't get any heat.

Coming from personal experience, I can't identify with this struggle more. Growing up, I would see people making fun of my mom and I for wearing our traditional outfits when we would go out for parties. However, when I see the others wear it, I hear people giving them the greatest compliments. And that doesn't make sense to me. Why are they being exotic and creative, while I am being ridiculed for embracing an aspect of my culture?

When Selena Gomez wore that bindi and decided to go on stage and dance to a song in which the lyrics do not go with the music at all, she was insulting every single South Asian woman. This is cultural appropriation. It is no different from adorning Native American moccasins and headdresses. If you have ever taken a history class, you know how badly the Native Americans were treated because of their culture, a culture that was very different from the Western culture. They were tortured, asked to abandon their heritage, and assimilate into the white dominant culture.

So today, when people from the dominant culture decide to wear those clothes and try to be exotic and treat them like Halloween costumes, it is offensive. The argument that people are just "honoring" them is ridiculous because at one time in American history, the natives were considered filth.

In the same way, trying to adopt the Indian culture while not understanding the significance of that culture is wrong. It is important to think twice before wearing garments and other objects of another culture; it is necessary to understand that these items can really mean something to the people of that culture.

EVALUATING THE AUTHOR'S ARGUMENTS:

In this viewpoint Fatima Farha makes the case that people should only wear a bindi if it is part of their families' culture. Do you agree with her reasoning? Using examples from her writing, explain why or why not? How does this compare to other examples of cultural appropriation?

Cultural Sharing Isn't Something to Be Discouraged

"There's a tough balance between co-opting traditions and voluntarily sharing customs."

Liz Wolfe

In the following viewpoint Liz Wolfe argues that white restaurant owners accused of appropriating another culture's food are not to blame for the systemic racism that has been in place for much of US history. The author asserts that instead of encouraging an environment of shaming people for missteps that are labeled as appropriation, we should use such mistakes as learning opportunities. She goes on to say that much good can be gained from exposure to other cultures and that cries of appropriation could scare people into stifling such exposure. Wolfe is managing editor of Young Voices.

AS YOU READ, CONSIDER THE FOLLOWING QUESTIONS:

1. Why were the owners of a Portland taco truck pilloried for trying to be authentic?
2. What did the author learn by visiting a white-owned Burmese restaurant?
3. According to the author, if white ownership of businesses isn't the problem, what is?

"The White-Owned Restaurant Outrage Is Wildly Misplaced," by Liz Wolfe, Foundation for Economic Education, May 26, 2017. https://fee.org/articles/the-white-owned-restaurant-outrage-is-misplaced/ Licensed under CC BY 4.0 International.

The latest political correctness outcry is a series of "white-owned appropriative restaurants" in Portland. While there are legitimate grievances to be made against white people who mock other cultures and then use them to profit once they become trendy, tirades like this list don't level the economic playing field. More often than not, they breed resentment as political correctness fights tend to back people into their respective partisan corners.

I read all the articles listed on the first page of the list—I should educate myself about hardships other people face while I remain immune. I'll give credit where it's due: many of these articles center around the idea that systemic disadvantage creates poverty, and many people of color don't have the same financial resources to open restaurants that their white counterparts have. It follows, then, that white people get to profit from rich cultural traditions while the people who have claim to that origin don't. I see how that feels viscerally unfair.

But are white entrepreneurs really the culprits here, or is it a larger system of historic disadvantage that has created these differences in wealth? Which system should we rebel against?

Appropriating Tortillas and Hip-Hop

Portland's Kooks Burritos food truck, one of the restaurants listed, recently closed their doors for good, presumably as a result of all the hate they'd been getting. In a profile by the Willamette Week, founders describe being entranced by the tortillas they had on a trip to Mexico. This inspired them to ask local ladies about the ingredients, but they would only reveal part of the recipe, not the techniques, leading the two Kooks founders to peek into windows of nearby restaurants attempting to learn the art of tortilla-making. Two white women spying on resistant Mexican cooks to open a trendy food truck sparked outrage.

There's a tough balance between co-opting traditions and voluntarily sharing customs. Perhaps the owners of Kooks Burritos erred too far on the side of co-opting, as they attempted to steal recipes from locals instead of engaging in voluntary exchange. But demonizing them is yet another foolish battle that won't right the wrongs of the past or teach fruitful lessons to white restaurant owners.

Is there a difference between the stereotypes celebrated by a German beer garden versus, say, a Mexican or Asian restaurant?

Cultural sharing isn't something to be intrinsically discouraged. Appropriation, as a concept, often seems logically inconsistent. When an American university fraternity tried to throw a theme party with a play on the song "Bad and Boujee," administrators objected, citing "cultural appropriation" as the problem. But which culture are we talking about? Which people are being subjugated and what is the true origin? "Latin, French, Marxist, Urban hip-hop?"

suggested Catherine Rampell at *The Washington Post*. In other words, is any iteration apart from the true origin an offensive act?

I doubt it. When we wade down the slippery slope of condemning people for well-intentioned practices, we often create enemies and become a culture where people are brutally shamed for their missteps, never learning from their mistakes.

How does this work when practices like yoga come under fire? Is yoga a less heinous thing to take part in because the origin is often explained more thoroughly? Perhaps yoga classes in US-based ashrams should continue to exist, but what about my less-conscious local YMCA? And still, who should make these judgment calls?

Using these Opportunities for Good

There seems to be a lot of gray area, and I doubt attempts to exercise more control over the individual would create good outcomes. Generally speaking, let's reserve use of authority and force for the direst situations in which people are directly harming one another.

A hardline reaction either way is misguided. The truth likely lies somewhere in the middle—marginalized groups have been historically disadvantaged, and that disadvantage often remains for many decades. But cultural appropriation isn't necessarily bad, nor is it as easily defined, as social justice advocates might hope. It's through cultural sharing, in its many forms, that people are able to make a living, spread knowledge of a particular topic, and advance current practices.

If a white business owner is spreading popularity of Burmese food, for example, and creating more demand for it, could that be a good thing for hopeful Burmese immigrants intent on entering the industry?

I went to a white-owned Burmese restaurant in Thailand where the owners had pamphlets on current events—namely the ethnic cleansing that has gripped much of the country. Although my appetite was reduced, exposure to Burmese culture made me more invested in Burmese current events. Now, headlines stick out to me. I remind traveler friends that they should be conscious of where their tourism money goes, as much of it unintentionally ends up lining the pockets of corrupt government officials.

White ownership isn't the problem in Portland. Instead, it's a complex web of systemic disadvantage, fear of ignorance on the part of proprietors, and worries that hard-working immigrants will be shoved out of the market. Those are more than worth fixing, but filing this cleanly under the "cultural appropriation" label doesn't give proper weight to the many sides of this important issue.

Let's stop condemning the wrong practices.

EVALUATING THE AUTHOR'S ARGUMENTS:

Viewpoint author Liz Wolfe makes a case for giving people the benefit of the doubt before systematically pillorying them for cultural appropriation. Do you agree with her perspective, or do you feel like she should take a hard stance one way or the other?

Viewpoint

5

Yoga Has Been Appropriated in the West

Maisha Z. Johnson and nisha ahuja

"A compassionate healing practice like yoga has to go through a lot of changes to fit a system of capitalism and white supremacy."

In the following viewpoint Maisha Z. Johnson and nisha ahuja argue that the sacred practice of yoga has been bastardized, commodified, and monetized in the West. The authors carefully explain how yoga has been culturally appropriated, as well as the harm that creates. This does not mean people in the West should not practice yoga, but they should understand the roots of yoga, what is sacred, and what is offensive and to be avoided. Johnson is the Digital Content Associate and Staff Writer of Everyday Feminism. ahuja is co-founder and co-director of Soma Ayurveda + Integrative Wellness.

AS YOU READ, CONSIDER THE FOLLOWING QUESTIONS:

1. How is yoga in the West an example of cultural appropriation?
2. In what way has yoga always impacted oppressed peoples according to the authors?
3. What is wrong with using sacred objects for purposes of authenticity according to the viewpoint?

"8 Signs Your Yoga Practice Is Culturally Appropriated—And Why It Matters," by Maisha Z. Johnson and nisha ahuja, Everyday Feminism, May 25, 2016. Reprinted by permission.

What draws you to yoga?

If you're reading this article, I'm guessing there's something about it that appeals to you. Is it how it makes your body feel? The chance to do something good for yourself? The way it helps you get centered?

Every year, more and more people are learning about the benefits of a yoga practice, and that can be wonderful.

And, as yoga gets more popular in mainstream culture, more and more people who aren't connected to the practice's roots are picking it up.

In the US, for example, the image of yoga is often associated with white, thin, able-bodied, middle class women. If you're one of these women, yoga is being marketed to you all over the place, and might not have noticed anything wrong with the way it's being advertised.

If you're white, there's not necessarily anything wrong with you doing yoga. You're probably just doing it for your own wellness, so it might be strange to think you could be hurting anyone else.

The problem lies not with you doing the practice, but with how yoga is commonly practiced and commercialized in Western contexts like the US.

Cultural appropriation is a process that takes a traditional practice from a marginalized group and turns it into something that benefits the dominant group—ultimately erasing its origins and meaning.

And that's exactly what's happening with yoga in Western spaces. The practices are based on traditions that go back thousands of years in South Asia and other places around the world, including East Africa's Kemetic Yoga. But this context and much of the essence of yoga's meaning has been stripped away.

This has a damaging impact—though I know you don't mean to cause any harm. So let's unpack the impact of culturally appropriative yoga, so that you can figure out how to make sure you're not contributing to harm.

I've spoken with nisha ahuja, an accomplished justice educator and facilitator who is known for her work addressing cultural appropriation of traditional healing practices.

This information offers nisha's wisdom and the knowledge of those who have informed her work, and it's an invitation for you to

Yoga has been commercialized and commodified in the west. But that doesn't mean it's wrong to engage in the practice.

deepen your understanding of yoga practices and how they relate to building a more equitable world.

nisha speaks from a South Asian context, with yoga practiced as medicine and a spiritual path in places like India for thousands of years. All over the world, similar healing practices have existed in places that were colonized.

You can find more acknowledgments at the end of the piece, but nisha would particularly like to give thanks to collaborator and contributor Melissa Moore, a Black and Cherokee justice, healing, and Dharma practitioner; friends, community, and colleagues who are Black, Indigenous, Non-Caste Privileged South Asians, cash-poor, disabled, and abundant bodied; and members of Bending Towards Justice and Brown Girls Yoga.

nisha wants to be clear that this isn't about reclaiming yoga for Hindus as some right wing extremism calls for—that's counteractive to the work. It's about understanding the complexities of oppression within the Western context of your yoga practice.

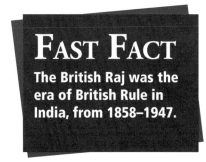

Even within a South Asian context, yoga incorporated practices from Indigenous peoples and those who would later be excluded through the caste system, which most often goes uncredited—so yoga that's exclusionary has always had a negative impact on the oppressed.

And this is only the beginning of how cultural appropriation can cause harm. If you're able to notice when this is happening, then you can continue to build your yoga practice in a way that benefits you and helps you avoiding harming other people.

Here are some signs of cultural appropriation to watch out for—and some ideas for how to build a more healing practice.

1. You're Treating Yoga Like a Solely Physical Activity

Many people think of yoga as a type of exercise, and nothing more.

If physical health is all you get out of your yoga practice, you deserve to be able to take care of your body. But it is important to know that the physical aspect of yoga isn't all there is to it—and in most lineages of yoga, the physical component is just a small fraction of the practice.

Yoga is also a spiritual path—and the story of how it got turned into the form of exercise you know today isn't a pretty one.

Through colonial suppression of Yogic practice and spirituality during the British Raj, one could be violently persecuted for not converting to Christianity or for publicly promoting Yogic teachings.

This catalyzed a coercion towards Western style athletics and aesthetics, so "turn of the century" (1800s to 1900s) body building and showmanship culture in some lineages of yoga were reemerging publicly. Many lineages maintained the deep spiritual practices, but had to keep these teachings private for fear of violent repercussions.

Throughout the history of colonization, demonizing the spiritual practices of Indigenous people and people of color is part of how colonizers have justified violence against them.

Those practices have played an essential role in many people's healing, health, and survival. So it's important that we don't redefine yoga as a solely physical practice.

Doing so relies on racist thinking—legitimatizing what white and Western people like about yoga, and invalidating its original meaning.

Many of the yogic teachings that were brought to the West were done so with this continual colonial coercion, with a need to appease and appeal to the Western mind by making connections of yoga to Christianity and/or defining it as a physical activity.

So if you want to do physical exercises based on yoga practices, it's possible to do that without contributing to oppressive ideas. Just acknowledge that you're only doing the physical practices.

By specifying that this is an exercise derived from yoga practices—not the entire practice of yoga itself—you can avoid mischaracterizing what yoga is all about.

2. The Practice Includes Shame and Ridicule

Going hard and pushing yourself in order to get a good workout works for some people, but it's not for everyone.

And when "pushing yourself" means being shamed for your body or abilities, it can take a toll on your sense of self-worth.

Shame is not part of the practice of yoga. But some studios operate as if getting "hot," straining to the brink of exhaustion, and feeling humiliated is what yoga is all about.

So what does this mean for your practice? Well, if it's stressing you out, then it's not what yoga is meant to be.

As is central in yogic practices, there should be compassion, not ridicule, and a sense of internal ease, instead of poses that cause your body stress.

You can honor the pace that's best for your body, instead of over-exerting yourself.

3. You're Not Acknowledging Where the Practices Come From

Neglecting to recognize the origins of what you're using is a classic sign of cultural appropriation.

You may not mean to participate in the system of white supremacy by doing this, but it's part of how the system operates—by removing any trace of people of color from the positive things we create.

So if you get on board with "yoga" that's marketed as a hot, New Age trend, you're supporting a business model based on theft and disrespect for a thousands-year-old history.

Maybe you're wondering: What does this long history have to do with you practicing yoga today?

Well, humbleness and humility are foundations of a yoga practice. Through interconnectedness, you recognize that you didn't come up with these practices all on your own. You show respect to the teachers who have come before you, and the people they learned from.

You can approach your own practice with humility, and look out for it in your yoga teachers, too.

If the person leading your session is put up on a pedestal without any acknowledgment of the people or regions that yoga practices come from, they're contributing to destroying the lineages that many folks are fighting to protect.

You can try talking to them about acknowledging the origins of yoga in the practice—or consider supporting another space that's more grounded in yoga's roots.

4. You're Misusing Sacred Objects

Hopefully, if you and your yoga teachers knew the significance of sacred objects, you wouldn't intentionally use them in disrespectful ways.

But lots of people include sacred objects in their yoga practice without realizing the significance of what they're using.

Sometimes, it's an attempt to give an "authentic" flare to a yoga studio—but misusing a sacred object as nothing more than a piece of décor is a dead giveaway that you don't have a real grasp of authenticity.

Anyone who uses a cultural item they're not familiar with should do their research to understand where it comes from, what it means, the protocols of engaging with and utilizing it, and how it should be cared for.

For instance, anything used in healing or spiritual practices—like scriptures, crystals, and statues of Buddha—is meant to be treated with respect.

If you use these objects for your own purposes, you're not respecting them or the cultures they come from. You're just exotifying and fetishizing other cultures without really understanding them.

For comparison, you probably wouldn't use pages of a Bible as decoration without understanding anything about Christianity.

So if you spot a sacred item on the ground or being used for toilet decoration in a yoga studio, you might want to have a word with the staff.

They don't have to know everything about the items they're using—but they should make an effort to have someone around who has that knowledge or is learning.

5. You're Not Being Accountable When Speaking Sacred Languages

Many Western yoga spaces treat sacred languages the same way they treat sacred items—without knowledge or respect for what they're using.

For instance, you might use Sanskrit, or chant without knowing what you're saying or why.

Sound can be healing, and you don't necessarily need to learn a whole new language to get something out of chanting. But, just like with the sacred objects, you could have a harmful impact if you use language without understanding its significance.

It can be hurtful for South Asian people to hear their traditional languages being misused, butchered, and even laughed at.

In a South Asian context, Sanskrit is caste exclusionary. There may be people in the room who have been affected by that system of inequality, and your use of the language could be the opposite of healing for them.

When nisha is leading a yoga session and she uses Sanskrit, she lets people know that they're going to use it and what they're going to be saying. She contextualizes the caste and religious divides that Sanskrit has and can create, and shifts the intention of using Sanskrit to engage the energy channels of our physical and subtle bodies.

Pay attention to how your yoga practice treats sacred texts, languages, and chants.

6. A White Person Who Ignores Oppression Is Leading the Practice

Avoiding cultural appropriation isn't about getting white people to stop participating in yoga or leading yoga sessions. But when the only option for studying yoga is to learn from a white person who ignores the complexities of oppression, that's a problem.

And that's happening in yoga spaces where white teachers don't acknowledge or address how white supremacy can show up and marginalize people of color.

For instance, there are lots of opportunities for people who fit the mainstream image of the industry—thin, white, middle class women—to get funding, space, and respect as leaders deemed experts.

As a result, for a South Asian or Black person trying to access yoga teachings from South Asia or Africa, it takes a lot of work to find an authentic connection with a teacher who is carrying on the traditions—not just leading a diluted form of them.

On the other hand, people who are working to create more inclusive spaces, like nisha, face barriers in getting support from a white-centered industry.

That doesn't mean it's wrong for you to support a white yoga facilitator. But you can recognize how the industry marginalizes those who don't fit the mainstream image of "modern" Western yoga.

All kinds of folks are being excluded. Not only teachers, but also practitioners who are poor, people of color, disabled, transgender and non-binary, fat, and more.

To be more inclusive of people who don't fit the dominant norm, white leaders need to recognize why marginalized people don't feel welcome and commit to do something about it.

If your teacher is a white person who fetishizes the practices without acknowledging where they're from, there's a good chance that they're not committed to recognizing their privilege and minimizing their harm in the world.

Some teachers present themselves as experts on South Asianness or yoga—and it's a problematic trend of white supremacy to center them as the experts, rather than trusting and elevating the knowledge of people who are actually part of these cultures.

As a consumer of this industry, you can show your support for respectful engagement with yoga practices by seeking out facilitators who are respectful in their practice.

7. You're Treating Yoga Like a Commodity

A compassionate healing practice like yoga has to go through a lot of changes to fit a system of capitalism and white supremacy.

So you know you're getting a culturally appropriated version of yoga when it's all about the money.

Think of yoga accessories and fashion lines that big corporations profit from, or studios aiming to make as much money as possible.

Yoga practices are about sustaining ourselves in ways that have nothing to do with money or material possessions. When it turns into something that's sellable, it loses its sacred value.

Unfortunately, treating the cultures of people of color this way, especially Black and Indigenous peoples, is a common trend in the US. Cultural appropriation strips the essence of our cultures away, reducing it to something the dominant culture can use for profit and entertainment.

Meanwhile, anything that can't be turned into a profit isn't considered valuable.

Yoga practices can help us reconnect with the parts of ourselves that oppression tries to get rid of. So be wary of spaces that treat yoga as a trendy possession to be bought and sold.

Those cute matching accessories might be calling your name. But if they're calling you to give your money to a corporation that's not supporting a traditional yoga practice, that purchase could have a negative impact.

You can help preserve traditional yoga practices by engaging with them outside of that commercialized mold.

8. You're Only Thinking About Your Own Personal Gain

How do you benefit from yoga?

Maybe the practice has had a positive influence on your mental health, your body, or your personal life. Taking care of yourself is such an important act of self-love, and we don't get encouragement to show love to ourselves nearly often enough.

So when people ask you to avoid appropriation, you might think they're saying you have to give up thinking about your own self-care altogether.

That's not what we're saying. It's awesome that you can show yourself love through yoga practices.

And you have the opportunity to shift the oppressive pattern that so many of us are taught to follow—the one that encourages you to take what benefits you on the surface without considering the impact on other people.

A system that only values you for your bank account doesn't actually value who you really are.

But an authentic yoga practice can help you grow as your whole self—mind, body, and spirit. Embracing your wholeness includes recognizing that you are part of a big, beautiful collective of other beings.

Thinking of others gives you a chance to think twice before feeling entitled to take from them for your own personal gain. If you're using something in your self-care practice that didn't originate in your culture, do some research so you don't adopt this practice in a way that harms people.

Try opening up to the compassionate side of a yoga practice. Include your love for yourself and consideration for others by avoiding appropriation, learning about the roots of yoga, and supporting inclusive spaces.

Why the Appropriation of Yoga Matters

If these signs of cultural appropriation are familiar to your yoga practice, that doesn't mean you're a bad person.

We're all taught to follow the systems of oppression that dominate our society, and every one of us has to go through a learning process to decolonize our thoughts and behaviors.

If you're doing yoga for reasons as personal as getting in touch with your own body, I understand why you may be confused about about this issue. Are you really hurting anyone?

Here's some background info on why the appropriation of yoga is important to think about.

The word "yoga" comes from a word meaning "union"—which explains that connection you feel between mind, spirit, and body.

And yoga practices also include the connection between yourself and others, for collective healing and liberation. That means being thoughtful about your impact on others as you move through the world.

Cultural appropriation is a perfect example of how you can cause harm if you're not thoughtful about your impact in the world.

If you think only of yourself and how you benefit from practicing yoga, it's possible that you'll inadvertently further marginalize the people of the cultures that it comes from. But if you consider that your behavior can affect other people, you'll take into account the history and context of what happens when yoga is appropriated.

For an example, let's talk about what that looked like in South Asia—though that's not the only origin of yoga, and it's important to remember, for instance, its African roots as well.

The British used violence, rape, and murder to take control of the South Asian sub-continent—and they approached yoga with violence, too. They forced people to convert to Christianity, and outlawed the healing and spiritual practices seen as "primitive" traditions, like yoga.

So how did South Asian and African people preserve yoga through all of that? With incredible resilience—and also by taking huge risks, with many of them losing their land and their lives.

With yoga being so popular these days, it's hard to imagine having to go through all of that just to practice it.

But unfortunately, this history has left a legacy of racism and domination that continues in Western approaches to yoga today.

Erasing and exotifying the South Asian and African roots is part of the story of how yoga was originally brought to Westerners.

After being demonized as a "savage" characteristic of the cultures of people of color, yoga was then repackaged in some schools as something white people could enjoy for entertainment and competition's sake.

These racist double standards still exist, as South Asian in Western places people are mistreated when they follow their cultural traditions, while white people gain profits, attention, and credit for using diluted versions of the same practices.

This is why it's dangerous to accept yoga as it's presented in mainstream images and marketing. There's so much more to it than the diluted version that's being sold to us.

Not only are you missing out on part of the practice—by buying into the mainstream industry's version of yoga, you're also only viewing yoga through a Western lens. This lens distorts what yoga is supposed to be, and adds racism, exotification, and exclusivity.

The more the practice of yoga is dominated by this commercialized distortion, the more society invalidates the authentic healing practices of people of color.

So those deep yoga practices that helped many South Asian and African people and other folks of color survive colonization and continue to help them survive marginalization today? Those are getting harder and harder to access, which means vital information about healing medicine is being lost.

If someone points out that you could do your yoga practice differently to help avoid this harm, consider it a gift. As nisha puts it, "It's a gift to learn how to love bigger."

With authentic yoga practices, you can love bigger, grow your compassion for yourself and others, and have a positive impact that radiates brilliantly through the world.

EVALUATING THE AUTHOR'S ARGUMENTS:

Viewpoint authors Maisha Z. Johnson and nisha ahuja use an instructive tone and are careful to assuage any guilt the reader might feel. Is their approach of gentle correction effective? How might you have received the content of this viewpoint if the authors had harshly criticized Westerners for practicing yoga?

Facts About Cultural Appropriation

Editor's note: These facts can be used in reports to add credibility when making important points or claims.

Culture can be defined as the social behaviors, norms, arts, and other manifestations of human societies.

Cultural studies is a field of research and teaching. It investigates the ways in which culture creates and changes people's experiences, everyday life, social relationships, and power.

Cultural exchange broadly refers to any mutual sharing of information between two or more groups. With cultural exchange, the purpose is to improve understanding and friendship between the groups. Cultural exchange programs may help students, artists, athletes, or others visit each other's countries.

Cultural appropriation is a term used to describe one cultural group taking creative or artistic practices from another. It usually describes Western appropriations of nonwestern or nonwhite practices. The term suggests exploitation, dominance, or racism. According to Oxford Reference, the concept was discussed by the 1970s, although the term cultural appropriation was not used until later.

To many people, cultural exchange is positive and cultural appropriation is negative. Cultural appropriation results from a power imbalance. Someone from a dominant group takes the clothing, accessories, music, etc. from a less powerful group. The dominant group may benefit financially and not share the money with the marginalized group or person. Someone in the dominant group may be praised for being fashionable or trendy for wearing an item from another culture. Meanwhile, someone expressing his or her historical culture may be criticized as old-fashioned or accused of not fitting in. This double standard or power imbalance lies at the heart of cultural appropriation.

Accusations of cultural appropriation have hit celebrities, companies, and ordinary individuals. Cultural appropriation charges have been laid against sports teams, fashion designers, musicians, visual artists, and many others. People have been accused of cultural appropriation for wearing Halloween costumes based on stereotypes of a different cultural group. People have also been accused of cultural appropriation for wearing hair styles, jewelry, and other accessories from outside their culture. Some people feel that white people should never wear items from marginalized cultures. Other people feel that whether the behavior is appropriate comes down to circumstances and intent.

Assimilation is the condition of being absorbed into something. Cultural assimilation happens when a minority group or culture comes to resemble a dominant group. This could mean taking on the language, clothing and hairstyles, diet, and customs of the dominant culture. Assimilation can be forced to the point of driving the minority culture into extinction. The deliberate and systematic destruction of a culture is called ethnocide.

Privilege refers to advantages people have based on their physical selves, rather than any earned merit. When a certain group has privilege due to its race or culture, this indicates a racist society. People can be privileged in some areas and not in others. The concept of privilege originally developed in discussions of race and gender. It has expanded to include sexual orientation, gender identification, social class, ability level, and other aspects of identity. People cannot choose whether they have privilege. However, people who are aware of their privilege can use their power to help others.

Explicit bias refers to the attitudes we have about a person or group on a conscious level. People can control how they express explicit bias. They may hide these biases in order to be more socially acceptable. For example, someone might think racist thoughts but choose not to express them aloud.

Implicit bias refers to attitudes that affect our understanding, decisions, and actions in an unconscious manner. They happen without our awareness or control. One can have implicit bias about many characteristics, such as race, ethnicity, age, and appearance. The news, social media, marketing, and life experiences can all affect implicit bias. Some programs have been developed to help people identify and eliminate their implicit biases.

Organizations to Contact

The editors have compiled the following list of organizations concerned with the issues debated in this book. The descriptions are derived from materials provided by the organizations. All have publications or information available for interested readers. The list was compiled on the date of publication of the present volume; the information provided here may change. Be aware that many organizations take several weeks or longer to respond to inquiries, so allow as much time as possible for the receipt of requested materials.

American Civil Liberties Union (ACLU)
125 Broad Street, 18th Floor
New York, NY 10004
(212) 549-2500
contact page: https://www.aclu.org/general-feedback
website: www.aclu.org
The ACLU works "to defend and preserve the individual rights and liberties guaranteed by the Constitution and laws of the United States." The website discusses many rights issues and links to online publications.

Echoing Ida
300 Frank H. Ogawa Plaza, Suite 700
Oakland, CA 94612
(510) 663-8300
website: https://forwardtogether.org/programs/echoing-ida
Echoing Ida's goal is to amplify Black women and nonbinary writers as experts in media. The website includes writings on a variety of subjects, such as Media & Culture, Health, and Sexuality.

GroundSpark
4104 24th Street, Suite 2013
San Francisco, CA 94114
(800) 405-3322

email: info@groundspark.org
website: https://groundspark.org/
GroundSpark's mission is "to create visionary films and dynamic educational campaigns that move individuals and communities to take action for a more just world." Learn about its projects and stream films online.

Intellectual Property Issues in Cultural Heritage Project (IPinCH)
Department of Archaeology
Simon Fraser University
8888 University Drive
Burnaby, British Columbia, Canada V5A 1S6
(778) 782-5709
fax: 778-782-5666
email: nicholas@sfu.ca
website: www.sfu.ca/ipinch/
The IPinCH research project is an international collaboration of archaeologists, anthropologists, indigenous organizations, and others. They work toward fair and equitable exchanges of knowledge relating to heritage. Learn about their Community Initiatives and find resources including fact sheets, publications, videos, and podcasts.

National Association for the Advancement of Colored People (NAACP)
4805 Mt. Hope Drive
Baltimore, MD 21215
(877) NAACP-98
email: actso@naacpnet.org
website: http://www.naacp.org/
The NAACP was founded in 1909. Its mission is "to ensure the political, educational, social, and economic equality of rights of all persons." Top issues include civic engagement, environment and climate justice, and health.

National Diversity Council
2401 Fountainview Drive, Suite 420
Houston, TX 77057
(281) 975-0626
contact form: http://www.nationaldiversitycouncil.org/contact/
website: www.nationaldiversitycouncil.org/
An organization dedicated to being a resource and an advocate for the value of diversity and inclusion. It offers education, mentoring, and leadership training.

The People's Institute for Survival and Beyond (PISAB)
601 N. Carrollton
New Orleans, LA 70119
(504) 301-9292
email: messages@pisab.org
website: https://www.pisab.org/
PISAB is a collective of anti-racist, multicultural community organizers and educators. The group is dedicated to building an effective movement for social transformation. It provides workshops to help people understand and challenge racism.

For Further Reading

Books

Brown, Michael F. *Who Owns Native Culture?* Cambridge, MA: Harvard University Press, 2004.

This title documents the efforts of indigenous people to reclaim their cultural property. It focuses on actual legal cases worldwide.

Crayton, Lisa A. *Everything You Need to Know about Cultural Appropriation* (Need to Know Library). New York City, NY: Rosen Young Adult, 2018.

This resource, targeted at teens, helps readers grasp the magnitude of cultural appropriation. It covers topics from clothing and jewelry to hairstyles and music.

Kopano, Baruti N., and Tamara Lizette Brown. *Soul Thieves: The Appropriation and Misrepresentation of African American Popular Culture* (Contemporary Black History). Basingstoke, UK: Palgrave Macmillan, 2014.

This collection of essays examines historical and contemporary examples of cultural appropriation of African American popular culture. Topics include music, dance, film, television, fashion, sports, and popular fiction.

Krings, Matthias. *African Appropriations: Cultural Difference, Mimesis, and Media* (African Expressive Cultures). Bloomington, IN: Indiana University Press, 2015.

The author explores the ways Africans have adapted cultural forms to their own purposes.

Scafidi, Susan. *Who Owns Culture?: Appropriation and Authenticity in American Law* (Rutgers Series: The Public Life of the Arts). New Brunswick, NJ: Rutgers University Press, 2005.

Who owns art forms? This book explores the question from a legal point of view. In addition, it asks questions about why some forms of work are legally protected and others are not.

Simon Fraser University. *Think Before You Appropriate: Things to know and questions to ask in order to avoid misappropriating Indigenous cultures—A guide for creators and designers.* Burnaby, BC, Canada: Simon Fraser University, 2016.

This 20-page guide contains advice geared to businesses wanting to use imagery from indigenous peoples. It is available online at http://www.sfu.ca/ipinch/sites/default/files/resources/teaching_resources/think_before_you_appropriate_jan_2016.pdf.

Young, James O. *Cultural Appropriation and the Arts.* Hoboken, NJ: Wiley-Blackwell, 2010.

A philosopher investigates the moral and artistic issues of cultural appropriation.

Young, James O., and Conrad G. Brunk. *The Ethics of Cultural Appropriation.* Hoboken, NJ: Wiley-Blackwell, 2012.

This title brings together a collection of essays from experts in the social sciences and philosophy. They examine the effects of cultural appropriation in the arts, religion, and more.

Ziff, Bruce. *Borrowed Power: Essays on Cultural Appropriation.* New Brunswick, NJ: Rutgers University Press, 1997.

A collection of essays on cultural appropriation, especially America's use of Native American culture.

Periodicals and Internet Sources

Anderson, Melinda D., "Can Science Help People Unlearn Their Unconscious Biases?," *Smithsonian Magazine*, January 9, 2017. http://www.smithsonianmag.com/science-nature/can-science-help-people-unlearn-their-unconscious-biases-180955789/.

Bajaj, Niya, "Culture Wars: appropriation vs. inclusion, and why it matters," *The Tête-à-Tête*, February 8, 2016. https://theteteatete.org/2016/02/08/culture-wars-appropriation-vs-inclusion-and-why-it-matters/.

Baker, Katie J.M., "A Much-Needed Primer on Cultural Appropriation," *Jezebel*, November 13, 2012. https://jezebel.com/a-much-needed-primer-on-cultural-appropriation-30768539.

Bradford, K. Tempest, "Commentary: Cultural Appropriation Is, In Fact, Indefensible," NPR, June 28, 2017. https://www.npr.org/sections/codeswitch/2017/06/28/533818685/cultural-appropriation-is-in-fact-indefensible.

Chen, Anna, "An American woman wearing a Chinese dress is not cultural appropriation," *Guardian*, May 4, 2018. https://www.theguardian.com/commentisfree/2018/may/04/american-woman-qipao-china-cultural-appropriation-minorities-usa-dress.

De Souza, Ruth, "Food and festivals: Consuming multiculturalism," Ruth De Souza blog, April 3, 2012. http://www.ruthdesouza.com/2012/04/03/food-and-festivals-consuming-multiculturalism/.

Galchen, Rivka, and Anna Holmes, "What Distinguishes Cultural Exchange from Cultural Appropriation?" *New York Times*, June 8, 2017. https://www.nytimes.com/2017/06/08/books/review/bookends-cultural-appropriation.html.

Krayewski, Ed, "A U.N. Effort to Make Cultural Appropriation Illegal?" *Reason*, June 14, 2017. https://reason.com/blog/2017/06/14/a-un-effort-to-make-cultural-appropriati.

Laneri, Raquel, and Connie Wang, "Ralph Lauren Runs An Assimilation-Themed Campaign," *Refinery 29*, December 18, 2014. https://www.refinery29.com/en-us/ralph-lauren-native-appropriation.

Lehmann, Claire, "The Evils of Cultural Appropriation," *Tablet*, June 11, 2018. https://www.tabletmag.com/jewish-news-and-politics/263933/cultural-appropriation.

Malik, Kenan, "In Defense of Cultural Appropriation," *New York Times*, June 14, 2017. https://www.nytimes.com/2017/06/14/opinion/in-defense-of-cultural-appropriation.html.

Olivia, Aarti, "11 Of the Most Culturally Appropriated South Asian Accessories, and What They Really Mean," Wear Your Voice, November 10, 2015. https://wearyourvoicemag.com/more/culture/11-culturally-appropriated-indian-accessories.

Smith, Andy, "For All Those Who Were Indian in a Former Life," People's Paths. http://www.thepeoplespaths.net/articles/formlife.htm.

Stahl, Aviva, "How Do We Unlearn Racism? Complex Life," Complex, November 9, 2016. http://www.complex.com/life/2016/11/how-do-we-unlearn-racism.

Steele, Marjorie, "Why I'm done nail-biting about cultural appropriation," *Creative Onion*, August 4, 2017. https://creativeonion.me/why-im-done-nail-biting-about-cultural-appropriation-8608edf-291cc.

Thorpe, JR, "Can You Unlearn Racism By Re-training Your Brain?," *Bustle*, September 20, 2016. https://www.bustle.com/articles/184790-can-you-unlearn-racism-by-re-training-your-brain.

Tylt, "In Defense of Cultural Appropriation," Tylt, https://thetylt.com/culture/does-cultural-appropriation-even-matter.

Websites

Bias Cleanse (www.lookdifferent.org/what-can-i-do/bias-cleanse)
MTV's "Look Different" campaign and the Kirwan Institute for the Study of Race and Ethnicity created seven-day "bias cleanses." The daily tasks are designed to help people change their conscious and unconscious biases. Cleanses for race, gender, and anti-LGBTQ bias are available.

Decolonization: Indigeneity, Education & Society (jps.library.utoronto.ca/index.php/des)
This scholarly journal publishes articles on work engaged in decolonization. Decolonization is the undoing of colonialism.

Groundwork for Change (groundworkforchange.org)
The site gathers information "to help non-Indigenous/settler peoples grow relationships with Indigenous peoples that are rooted in solidarity and justice. The site is meant to support people who are asking questions and looking to learn more in respectful and useful ways."

Native Appropriations (nativeappropriations.com/)
This site provides a forum for discussing representations of Native peoples, including stereotypes and cultural appropriation.

RACE: Are We so Different? (www.understandingrace.org)
This website is a project of the American Anthropological Association. It looks at race through three different lenses: history, human variation, and lived experience. It offers activities for students plus resources.

The Storytelling Project Curriculum (www.racialequitytools.org/resourcefiles/stp_curriculum.pdf)
The Storytelling Project Curriculum, created through Barnard College, analyzes race and racism in the United States through storytelling and the arts. The curriculum is designed for teachers but could be used by self-directed students.

Welcoming Schools (www.welcomingschools.org/resources/)
Welcoming Schools is a project of the Human Rights Campaign. It offers tools, lessons, and resources. Topics include embracing family diversity and ending bullying and name-calling in elementary schools.

Index

inclusion, 99, 100
interconnectedness, 97
meaning of, 93
origins, 93, 97, 101, 102
as physical activity, 95, 96
Sanskrit, 98–99
use of sacred objects, 97–98
Young, Marion, 18

Z
Zendaya, 46

Picture Credits

Cover Seb Oliver/Cultura/Getty Images; p. 11 Kevin Winter/Getty Images; p. 15 Superlime/Shutterstock.com; p. 19 Aleoks/Shutterstock.com; p. 26 RosaIreneBetancourt 12/Alamy Stock Photo; p. 32 Ollie Millington/Redferns/Getty Images; p. 39 miker/Shutterstock.com; p. 42 Bettmann/Getty Images; p. 45 Golden Pixels LLC/Shutterstock.com; p. 50 Sandra Foyt/Shutterstock.com; p. 54 The Boston Globe/Getty Images; p. 59 ValeStock/Shutterstock.com; p. 68 Bachmann Bill/Perspectives/Getty Images; p. 70 Sunshine/Alamy Stock Photo; p. 73 Patrick McDermott/Getty Images; p. 79 Dan Kitwood/Getty Images; p. 84 Victor Fraile/Getty Images; p. 89 Ronald Sumners/Shutterstock.com; p. 94 fizkes/Shutterstock.com